early
Sensory
Skills

early Sensory Skills

Jackie Cooke

Speechmark Publishing Ltd
8 Oxford Court, St James Road, Brackley, NN13 7XY, UK

JACKIE COOKE qualified as a speech therapist in 1983, at the School for the Study of Disorders of Human Communication (now part of the City University, London). For nearly ten years she worked with a variety of client groups, in a wide range of settings, within Lewisham and Southwark. Since 1986 she has specialized in the communication problems of children and adults with severe learning difficulties, becoming particularly interested in teaching social and sensory skills. In 1994 she gained an MSc in Human Communication from City University. She is joint author of *Working with Children's Language* (Speechmark Publishing, 1985).

For the sake of clarity alone, this text uses 'she' to refer to the child.

Published by

Speechmark Publishing Ltd, 8 Oxford Court, St James Road, Brackley, NN13 7XY, United Kingdom
Telephone: +44 (0)1280 845570   Facsimile: +44 (0)1280 845584
www.speechmark.net

002-3042/Printed in the United Kingdom/1010

British Library Cataloguing in Publication Data
Cooke, Jackie
   Early sensory skills. – (Early skills series)
   1. Sense and sensation in infants 2. Infant psychology
   3. Senses and sensation – Study and teaching
   I. Title
   155.4'22'21

ISBN 978 086388 371 2
(Previously published by Winslow Press Ltd under ISBN 0 86388 218 8)

EARLY SENSORY SKILLS
Contents

ACKNOWLEDGEMENTS

After many, many hours of toil and trouble, not the least of which has been wrestling with the intricacies of the personal computer, I finally feel in a position to thank the people who helped to make this book possible.

I am grateful to Diana Williams for her helpful comments in the early stages, to Debbie Parsons for typing the first draft, and to Stephanie Martin for her encouragement and belief in this project. My thanks also to David Doorly for once again supporting me throughout. Acknowledgements are due to Karen Bunning, from whose early work on sensory integration some of these activities were derived. Finally, a big thank-you to the staff and pupils of the special schools I have worked in, for encouraging and developing these activities — especially to the children, who taught me so much!

This book is dedicated to everybody I knew at Watergate School during the seven and a bit years that it was my pleasure to 'work' there.

INTRODUCTION

BACKGROUND

Who is this Manual for?

This manual is intended for anyone working with young children. It should be useful in the home, in therapy clinics, and in schools, nurseries and playgroups, including those catering for children with special needs.

How to Use this Manual

The manual is divided into sections on vision; touch; taste and smell; everyday activities; games; and topics. There is an introduction to each section, which includes the major principles and aims behind the activities. These are intended as background information to help in planning and implementing sensory programmes.

The first three sections contain basic activities which are intended to stimulate and develop the senses of vision, touch, taste and smell. They are most suitable for very young children, and children with language problems which are primarily due to a learning difficulty, a physical handicap or a sensory impairment. However, they can also be used with older children, as quick, 'fun' activities, to help them to learn the vocabulary associated with vision, touch, taste and smell, and to be more aware of these senses. Each activity sheet contains full instructions, as well as suggestions for variations and similar activities.

Any activities which may become messy carry a warning symbol.

The remaining three sections describe more familiar ways to stimulate the senses, through everyday activities, games and topics. Except for the everyday activities, these are intended for older or more able children.

A symbol is used to denote games which are suitable for groups.

The activity sheets, everyday activities and games can be photocopied and given out to parents, carers and support staff, under the guidance of a clinician or teacher.

Any important considerations or warnings are highlighted by the symbol.

Sections 1 to 4 have simple photocopiable checklists so that you can keep a record of a child's progress and interests. In Appendix I there is a list of useful items to collect for basic sensory work; Appendix II has the words to the songs that are used in the text; and Appendix III provides some useful addresses.

Useful Words

A short list of useful words is included with each basic activity. These can be used in two ways: first, as a topic vocabulary for the more able child to learn, and second, as a very consistent set of words and phrases that you would like the child to understand but do not expect her to use. This would be the case with infants and severely delayed children who have no speech.

The activities can also be carried out non-verbally, or with the minimum of speech. The vocabulary is meant only as a helpful guideline.

Take Care

If you intend to use these activities with physically handicapped children, it is essential that they are comfortable, with good seating and posture. Consult the appropriate professionals, such as physiotherapists, occupational therapists, speech and language clinicians and dieticians, especially before starting activities that involve tasting and eating.

Hints for Working with Children

1 The child should be alert, but content and comfortable, especially when you introduce new activities.

2 Establish a routine so that you can do some of these activities every day.

3 Get everything ready before you start.

4 Try and work in a quiet place, keeping distractions to a minimum.

5 Go at the child's pace — some activities will take less time than you think, others will take longer.

6 Take the child's lead as far as possible — you will make better progress.

7 Try and finish an activity before the child gets bored.

8 Only continue playing for as long as both you and the child are alert and enjoying the games. If *you* get bored, the child probably will too.

9 Above all, enjoy yourselves — these activities are meant to be for fun and relaxation, as well as to develop skills, so let yourself go!

Remember!

◆ Communicate with the child: chat, smile, play.

◆ Watch your own language level.

◆ Look out for the child's responses and react appropriately.

◆ Respect her choices.

◆ Carry out the activities regularly and frequently, but not for too long.

◆ Provide comfortable, relaxing surroundings.

◆ Be aware of all possible risks.

BASIC ACTIVITIES

Introduction

Very young infants use looking, touching, handling, mouthing, smelling and tasting to explore the objects they come into contact with. These actions provide valuable information about the world. Touching and handling remain important ways of interacting with the environment throughout our lives, while smelling and tasting also retain a key role. However, compared to vision, their contribution is often overlooked, especially for older children. We all learn about an object more quickly if we can touch it, as well as look at and listen to it.

Organization of Basic Activities

1 Make sure the child is comfortable and ready to play. There is no point in introducing activities if she is unhappy, hungry or uncomfortable.

2 Make sure she can be as fully involved as possible. She may be sitting, lying or standing, but needs to be able to see and touch the toys easily.

  If she is physically disabled you should seek appropriate advice. Some activities may be better suited to one position rather than another.

3 Try and reduce background noises and distractions, so that the child can concentrate on the activity.

  If you are working in a classroom or nursery, try to have an uncluttered area, without wall displays, that can be screened off from other children. If you are at home, try to have some time in the day without the radio or television on.

4 The best person to carry out these activities with the child is somebody who knows her well and whom she likes being with. This is usually a parent or carer, but these activities can also be used in schools, nurseries and clinics.

  If you are using these activities with a baby or less able child, a familiar person will be able to observe and interpret her responses more accurately.

5 Make sure that all the toys, objects and materials are safe and hygienic. A useful tip is to have a supply of antiseptic wipes available for quick on-the-spot cleaning, but you should not let this interfere with your play.

6　Be particularly aware of the dangers of electrical and mechanical equipment and keep it regularly cleaned and maintained. Trailing wires, accessible plugs and switches can pose a risk, so take all possible care!

Aims

The main focus for all the activities is on communication between the child and her helper. The child is given opportunities to interact with another person, to have interesting experiences and to make discoveries.

Through her responses to these experiences, and her helper's reactions to her responses, she should learn to express preferences, to make choices and to communicate, in any way she can, whether through speech or with body language. For instance, if a child pulls her hand away from a texture and the adult removes it, the child learns to have some choice and control over what happens to her. If the adult persists in putting her hand back, the child learns she has no control.

Responses

1　The activities may need frequent and constant repetition in order to develop a child's skills. Usually the younger or more handicapped a child is, the longer she will need to spend on an activity before she makes a response or expresses a preference.

2　If you are using these activities with children of limited language ability, you will need to observe their responses very carefully. There are many possible responses, including looking, eye-pointing, avoiding looking, facial expressions, different vocalizations, reaching, pointing, touching, body language and so on. You cannot force such responses, only provide experiences that may produce them.

3　You should try to react quickly to children's responses. For example, if a child cries when feeling some jelly, she probably does not like it, and you should remove the jelly. However, this does not mean you never try that activity again — instead, you should experiment with when, where and how you introduce the jelly next time: perhaps it was too cold, or it was presented too suddenly, or the child may have been feeling unwell or unhappy at the time.

4　Some responses are open to misinterpretation, and you should look for patterns and consistencies before deciding whether a child likes or dislikes an activity.

5　Keep an activity going for as long as the child is enjoying it, but vary it to maintain her attention. Once she has lost interest, you should stop the activity and either do something different or give the child a little rest before trying again.

6 Above all, respond to the child and take your lead from her. If you do not respond to her efforts to communicate, she will soon give up trying. Likewise, if you ignore her attempts to say 'no' to an activity, she will not be able to express preferences, make choices and have any control over her environment.

VISION

THIS SECTION is about the sense of sight and is divided into three parts: 'Looking at People', 'Looking at Self' and 'Looking at Objects'. Most of the activities are better suited for one-to-one work. This is especially true for very young children, or those with attention problems, physical disabilities or learning difficulties, who need a lot of help and encouragement.

The emphasis is on the child experiencing visual activities presented by the adult. The activities are intended to be an enjoyable and simple form of play, but they will also stimulate the child's senses and help her to make a relationship with the adult.

The child may be unable to do much for herself, or she may be quite active. She may try to reach for the toys and explore them, to make choices about what to play with, and to communicate. We hope that all children will progress from being a passive participant to being an active one.

You can also use the basic activities with older or more able children, in order to teach them the appropriate vocabulary. Use the activities as quick, 'fun' games or adapt them for 'science' experiments.

Aims

1 To stimulate the child and increase her awareness of her sense of vision.

2 To help develop spatial awareness.

3 To encourage eye-contact between the child and her carer.

4 To encourage interactions between the child and her carer.

5 To encourage communication between the child and her carer.

6 To build up concepts about objects.

7 To help learn appropriate vocabulary.

Remember!

◆ Always encourage the child's attempts to communicate.

◆ Try using the useful words provided.

◆ Respect her likes and dislikes.

◆ You should never force a child to look at something or someone. However, you can give physical assistance to a child who is having difficulty turning her head or looking in the right direction.

◆ Most of these activities are better suited for one-to-one work.

◆ Try to end the activities and games *before* the child gets bored.

◆ Keep all other distractions to a minimum when carrying out these activities; for example, don't have the television on!

◆ Seek advice from the appropriate professionals when working with children who are visually impaired, visually sensitive or who suffer from epilepsy, migraines and so on.

LOOKING AT PEOPLE

Looking at other people is an important skill. It helps us to learn to communicate, to understand what people are saying, to take turns in conversation or play, to get people's attention, to make friends and to develop good social skills.

Most children learn primarily through looking and watching. They then imitate what other people do, which helps them to try out and practise new skills. They can improve their skills through the feedback and reactions from adults and other children.

Eye-to-eye contact is particularly important for communication, whether by speech or signing, and for social interaction.

LOOKING AT PEOPLE ACTIVITIES
General Points

1   Try to keep the child's eye-contact going, but remember it is normal to look away from time to time, and it is not appropriate to look at someone for too long, or to stare.

2   If a child shows more interest in objects than in people, you can put her favourite toy next to your face to encourage her to look at you. Make the toy disappear after a little while so that the child finds herself looking at just your face. When she looks away, call her name and bring back the toy, to get her attention back. Gradually, take longer to make the toy reappear, so that eventually the child will look at you when you call her.

3   Use mealtimes in a similar way: that is, hold each spoonful up by your face for a second or two.

4   Do not leave the child on the floor where she cannot see you for long. When she is in her chair, move her around the room, so that she can keep you in her sight and also get a change of view.

5   Make sure she has toys and activities to stimulate her while you are occupied, but remember that people are her best playthings. Keep her where she can see your face and movements, and hear your voice. She will enjoy watching you, whatever you are doing.

LOOKING AT
PEOPLE ACTIVITIES
Lap-play

What to do

1 You can do this anywhere, even on a bus, if you don't mind people looking at you.

2 Sit the child securely on your lap, face-to-face.

3 Smile and chat, make faces and so on, to get her attention.

4 Gently sway from side to side with her.

5 Rock a little more vigorously, as much as she can take, while continuing to smile and make eye-contact.

Variations

◆ Sing lullaby songs.

◆ Wear eye-catching things, such as wigs or face make-up.

◆ Instead of rocking in the same direction as the child, rock in opposite directions, and make a big fuss or 'boo' her at the middle point where your faces meet again.

◆ Rock backwards and forwards instead of side to side.

◆ Bounce the child up and down, gently at first.

◆ Leave little pauses to build up her anticipation, but not so long that she starts to look away.

◆ Pretend to drop her or let her fall (if she can take this).

Similar activities

You can carry out similar activities with different games, as long as you stay facing each other.
For example:

◆ play rowboats (sit the child facing you on your lap or the floor, hold her hands or hug her, and rock back and forth); sing 'rowing' songs;

You will need:

*just your own lap
(and some energy).*

Useful words
and phrases:

*hello; I can see you;
let's cuddle; let's rock;
side-to-side; left; right;
here we go; and again;
finished; more;
words of any cradle
or rockabye songs
you want to sing.*

- tickle games, cuddles and kisses (on the child's face and fingers);
- finger rhymes and hand-games, such as 'Walkie round the garden';
- pat-a-cake and clapping games.

Some physical games are also suitable for keeping eye-contact, as they are played face-to-face. For example:

- jump the child up and down;
- swing her round and round in your arms;
- lift her up and pretend to drop her;
- push her on a swing;
- sit opposite each other on a seesaw.

LOOKING AT PEOPLE ACTIVITIES
Faces

What to do

1 You can do this anywhere, even on a bus, if you don't mind people looking at you.

2 As long as she can see your face, the child can be in almost any position, such as sitting on your lap or a chair, lying in bed or on the floor, and so on. Make sure you are both comfortable.

3 Smile and chat to get her attention. It doesn't matter what you are saying, as the movement of your lips will keep the child looking at your face.

4 Make faces, not too exaggerated at first, as you might look threatening. For example, raise your eyebrows, wrinkle your nose, make different shapes with your mouth, such as a wide surprised look, a smile, a little 'O', and so on.

5 If you lose the child's attention, either try a variation or change to another game.

Variations

◆ Shake your head or rock it from side to side.

◆ If you have long hair, shake it around and use it to hide your face.

◆ Bring your face close to the child's and move away again.

◆ Give kisses and cuddles.

◆ Zoom in towards the child's face and end with a kiss, a tickle or pretend to 'bite' the child's nose.

◆ Let the child touch your face.

◆ Stop chatting for a little while.

◆ Make sounds, such as blowing raspberries or kisses.

◆ Talk 'baby-talk' or sing.

◆ Hide your face, or just your eyes, with your fingers.

You will need:

just yourself.

Useful words and phrases:

hello; name of child; look; see my face?; here are/here's my eyes/nose/mouth/tongue; where are/where's your eyes, and so on.

Similar activities

You can carry out similar activities using objects and toys to attract attention to your face. For example:

Decorating your face:

◆ wigs, especially shiny or Day-Glo ones;

◆ masks (but make sure the child isn't frightened);

◆ face paints and make-up;

◆ glasses (you can buy giant-sized ones in many toyshops);

　　◆ big, dangly earrings and large necklaces (but be careful if the child is prone to grabbing things);

　　◆ colourful hats;

　　◆ you can buy an assortment of odd headgear, such as headbands with flashing lights, feather head-dresses, veils, crowns, luminous hairbands, 'deely-boppers' (shiny antennae with small balls on the end, popular in the 1980s);

◆ put stickers, transfers, gummed shapes or stars on your face;

◆ sprinkle glitter on your cheeks.

Around your face:

◆ blow bubbles;

◆ blow party-blowers, whistles or small musical instruments (but don't cover up your face);

◆ blow or shake a windmill;

◆ wave a balloon;

◆ shake a variety of toys, for example Christmas baubles, musical shakers, mobiles, bells, wind-chimes, puppets on sticks, flags, rattles;

◆ wiggle your fingers beside your face;

◆ put things on your head, pretend to balance them and drop them off — balls and beanbags are good;

◆ allow toys to 'appear' magically on top of your head, from behind your ear or on your nose, and so on — in other words, hide them in your hand until the last moment.

LOOKING AT PEOPLE ACTIVITIES
Hiding Games

What to do

1. You can do this anywhere, even on a bus, if you don't mind people looking at you.

2. As long as she can see your face, the child can be in almost any position, such as sitting on your lap or a chair, lying in bed or on the floor, and so on. Make sure you are both comfortable.

3. Smile and chat to get her attention.

4. Put on the hat and draw the child's attention to it. After a while, tilt the hat down over your eyes, lift it again and say, "Peep-bo!"

5. Do this several times, hiding for a little longer each time.

6. If you lose the child's attention, either try a variation or change to another game.

Variations

◆ Cover your whole face with the hat.

◆ Lift the hat on and off your head.

◆ Wear a really outrageous hat.

◆ Leave the hat over your face for a longer time and see if the child will try to take it off.

◆ Put the hat on the child, and play 'peep-bo' on her face instead of yours.

◆ If the child is happy to have her face covered, leave the hat over her face a little longer than usual, and see if she will try to take it off.

◆ Use sunglasses, a scarf, a piece of paper, a toy or anything else that comes to hand, instead of the hat — glittery cheerleaders' pom-poms are really eye-catching and cover the whole face (they can be bought from well-known children's superstores).

◆ If the child isn't ready for your complete disappearance, experiment with see-through and semi-see-through materials.

◆ Just hide behind your own hands or hair.

◆ Remember to vary what you say: for example, "hello; here I am; boo!" and so on.

You will need:

yourself; a hat (any kind, but a peaked or baseball cap is good).

Useful words and phrases:

hello; name of child; look; see my hat?; where's (your name) gone?; here I am; bye-bye; back again; on; off.

11

Similar activities

You can carry out similar activities using various props. You must keep the element of surprise, but also use repetition, so that the child will enjoy the game, but keep looking for you. For example:

◆ hide different parts of your body (but remember this will not keep a child's interest for as long as 'peep-bo' games with the face);

◆ go behind the child and peep your head back round at her;

◆ duck up and down behind a table or chair or peep from behind a door;

◆ hide and reappear from different positions — above, below, from the left or the right of the child.

LOOKING AT PEOPLE ACTIVITIES
Hands

What to do

1 You can do this anywhere, even on a bus, if you don't mind people looking at you.

2 As long as she can see you, the child can be in almost any position, such as sitting on your lap or a chair, lying in bed or on the floor, and so on. Make sure you are both comfortable.

3 Smile and chat to get her attention.

4 Bring your hands up near to your eyes and slowly cover them, keeping your fingers spaced so that the child can still see your face. After a second or two, show your eyes again, but keep your hands by your face.

5 Repeat this several times, still chatting and telling her what you are doing.

6 Make yours hands flutter across the child's field of vision to one side then the other. See if she will follow the movement.

7 Flutter your hands in opposite directions and see which way she looks.

8 If you lose her attention, either try a variation or change to another game.

Variations

◆ Wave and say "bye-bye" and pretend to go.

◆ Wave good-bye in everyday situations.

◆ Use gestures, such as holding out your arms for a hug, beckoning the child to come to you, and so on.

◆ 'Walk' your fingers towards the child, possibly ending up by tickling her.

◆ Wiggle your fingers in front of the child, say "I'm coming to get you" and pretend to 'take off' her nose or tickle her tummy.

◆ Build up the tension; for example say, "Where shall I get you — your tummy? No … your ears!"

◆ Play hand-games, such as 'Here's the church, here's the steeple'; 'Tommy Thumb'; 'Two little dickie-birds sitting on a wall' (see pp 160–1 for full words and actions).

You will need:

just yourself.

Useful words and phrases:

hello; name of child; look; here are my hands; see my fingers; where are your hands?

13

Section 1: Vision

Similar activities

You can carry out similar activities using objects and toys to attract attention to your hands. For example:

Decorating your hands:

◆ bright rings and bracelets;

◆ bright nail-varnish or paint on your nails;

◆ large white or colourful gloves;

◆ paint your hands with patterns or little people;

◆ glove puppets, finger puppets;

◆ tie bells around your wrist.

Using toys:

◆ wave toys such as flags, windmills, giant bubble wands, and so on;

◆ hold a large teddy or other soft toy, and walk him towards the child;

◆ ring bells, shake shakers, and so on;

◆ use mobiles and musical toys which work when you pull their strings;

◆ use 'pullalong' trucks, toy animals and so on.

LOOKING AT SELF

The child needs to become aware of her own body, in order to learn certain skills. These include developing body-image, spatial skills and learning about the distinction between herself and the rest of her environment.

LOOKING AT
SELF ACTIVITIES
Hiding Games

You will need:

just yourself.

**Useful words
and phrases:**

hello; name of child;
look; here's/here are
your hand/fingers;
uh-oh, it's/they've gone!;
here it is/here they are;
bye-bye hand; back again.

What to do

1 You can do this anywhere, even on a bus, if you don't mind people looking at you.

2 The child can be in almost any position, as long as she can see your face and the part of her body you are going to hide. She can sit on your lap or her chair, lie in bed or on the floor, and so on. Make sure you are both comfortable.

3 Smile and chat to get her attention.

4 Draw her attention to her own hand; for example, hold it in front of her face, play with her fingers, do 'Walkie round the garden' and so on.

5 After a little while, hide her hand inside yours and say, "Where's your hand gone?"

6 Uncover her hand and make a big fuss about 'finding' it.

7 Do this several times, hiding her hand for a little longer each time.

8 If you lose her attention, either try a variation or change to another game.

Variations

◆ When you 'find' the child's fingers again, kiss, suck or pretend to bite them, or tickle the palm of her hand.

◆ Play the game when getting the child dressed — pretend her hand is stuck in her sleeve.

◆ Cover her hand with a cloth or soft toy (which can also pretend to bite her).

◆ Play the 'pile up hands' game. This is when you put your hand over the child's hand, she puts her other hand on top of yours and you put your other hand on top, making a 'pile' of hands. Carry on doing this, getting faster and faster, until you are laughing too much to continue.

16

Early Sensory Skills

Similar activities

You can carry out similar activities using various props. You must keep the element of surprise, but also use repetition, so that the child enjoys the game, but can anticipate what is going to happen. For example:

◆ hide different parts of the child's body — toes and feet; tummy; face; head (with the face and head you can use a mirror so the child can watch herself disappear; without a mirror the activity is more 'now you *can* see, now you can't');

◆ turn getting dressed into a game — this makes it more relaxing and enjoyable for the child, especially when putting clothes over her head, which is often scary, or if her arm really does get stuck;

◆ sit in front of a large mirror and hide the child's head under a favourite soft toy, hat or small cloth;

◆ if the child is happy about being covered, or being unable to see, experiment with different ways of hiding her, for example, under a sheet, a shiny 'space-blanket', a multicoloured sari, or inside a box.

LOOKING AT
SELF ACTIVITIES
Mirrors

You will need:

a full-length mirror, big enough for the child to see you both.

Useful words and phrases:

hello; name of child; look; can you see yourself?; mirror; up and down we go!; where are your hands/toes/eyes and so on?; here they are!

What to do

1 Sit in front of the mirror, with the child on your lap, and bounce her up and down. (Remember: she should be facing the mirror so that she can see her own movements.)

2 Swing her from side to side.

3 Sit still and point out different parts of her body.

4 If you lose her attention, either try a variation or change to another game.

Variations

◆ Play all kinds of lap-games.
◆ Lift her arms up in the air.
◆ Lift up her legs or feet.
◆ Rub or pat her tummy.
◆ Play 'peep-bo' games.
◆ Give cuddles.
◆ Kiss or tickle different parts of her body and face.
◆ Name each body part as you touch it or draw attention to it.

Similar activities

You can carry out similar activities in front of the mirror, using various props. For example:

Decorating the child's face:

◆ wigs, especially shiny or Day-Glo ones;
◆ masks (but make sure the child isn't frightened);
◆ face paints and make-up;
◆ glasses (you can buy giant-sized ones in many toyshops);
◆ big, dangly earrings and large necklaces (but not if she is likely to pull them hard);
◆ colourful hats;

- you can buy an assortment of odd headgear, such as headbands with flashing lights, feather head-dresses, veils, crowns, luminous hairbands, 'deely-boppers' (shiny antennae with small balls on the end, popular in the 1980s);
- put stickers, transfers, gummed shapes or stars on her face;
- sprinkle glitter on her cheeks.

Around her face:

- blow bubbles;
- blow party-blowers at her;
- blow or shake a windmill;
- wave a balloon;
- shake a variety of toys, for example Christmas baubles, musical shakers, mobiles, bells, wind-chimes, puppets on sticks, flags, rattles;
- wiggle your fingers beside her face.

The rest of her body:

- put clothes on the wrong body parts, such as socks on her hands, hat on her foot, and so on;
- dress her up in fancy clothes;
- tie a balloon to her arm or leg, so she can see that she is making it move;
- move about in front of the mirror: for example, walk around, dance, spin around as you hold her in your arms;
- if she likes it, spray tepid water onto different parts of her body as she watches;
- play with toys, for example stacking toys or building bricks — she may look more at the toys themselves, but she will notice her own actions.

Looking at
People/Self
CHECKLIST

Child's name	

Date	Activity		Comments/Responses
	Looking at People	Lap-Play	
		Faces	
		Hiding Games	
		Hands	
	Looking at Self	Hiding Games	
		Mirrors	

LOOKING AT OBJECTS

Looking at objects and events in the environment is an important skill. It helps us to learn about the world: what things look like, how they work and what we can do with them. We also learn to match what an object looks like with the way it feels, the sound it makes, and so on.

Most children learn primarily through looking, watching and doing. They try out new skills and improve them through the feedback and responses they receive from adults and other children.

LOOKING AT OBJECTS
ACTIVITIES
General Points

1 Try to keep the child's attention on objects and events for as long as possible, but remember it is normal to look away from time to time, and eventually to get bored. Do not try to push an activity beyond this stage.

2 If a child shows more interest in people than in objects, you can put toys next to your face to encourage her to look at them. Lower your face or break eye-contact and stop chattering after a little while, so that the child finds herself looking at just the toy. When she looks away, call her name and look at her again, to get her attention back. Gradually, give less and less eye-contact or move the toy further from your face, so that eventually she will look more at the toy.

3 Remember that objects are not as interesting to young children as people are. You will need to use very eye-catching or meaningful toys to keep the child's attention.

4 Make sure you give the child enough variety in her environment. With a baby or toddler you can change the toys in her cot and pushchair from time to time, and fix pictures in her cot where she can see them. Also move her around so that she can see different things in the environment. If at school, remember to change the pictures and displays, and vary the available toys.

5 Make sure the child has toys and activities to stimulate her while you are occupied elsewhere, but remember that people are her favourite playthings. Do not leave her for too long; keep her where she can see and hear people nearby.

LOOKING AT OBJECTS ACTIVITIES
Movement

What to do

1. Sit or lay the child down, making sure you are both comfortable.

2. Shake or twirl the mobile to attract the child's attention and keep her interest.

3. If the mobile is hanging up, point to it and see if she can follow your finger.

4. Hold her near to the mobile and encourage her to touch it or reach towards it.

5. Chat to her while you play and talk about what the mobile is doing.

Variations

◆ Move the mobile around so it is nearer to or further away from the child.

◆ Change the position of the mobile so that the child has to look up, straight ahead or to the side.

◆ You can darken the room and shine a torch onto the mobile to catch the light.

◆ Try varying the background: for example, a plain white wall, a coloured sheet, a pattern, a mirror;

◆ Leave the child alone to explore the toy — you could fix up a wind source, such as an open window or a *safe* portable fan, to keep the mobile moving.

Similar activities

You can carry out similar activities with different kinds of equipment. For example:

Objects with random movement:
◆ mobiles;
◆ patterned discs, such as laser discs, spinning tops;
◆ balloons (try tying a balloon loosely to the child's wrist, so it moves when she moves);
◆ streamers;
◆ bubbles;
◆ pom-poms (such as cheerleaders use);

You will need:

an interesting mobile, either hung where the child can easily see it or held in your hand.

Useful words and phrases:

look; up there; what is it?; can you see the mobile?; there it goes; isn't it pretty?; it's blowing; (name of whatever is on the mobile: for example, birds, butterflies and so on).

23

- home-made toys and mobiles: for example, hang fir cones on strings to blow in the breeze, perhaps spraying them with gold or silver paint first;
- bobbing bath toys;
- snow-scene toys (you shake them and they fill with 'snow'; usually bought at Christmas);
- natural environmental effects, for example falling leaves, falling rain or snow, leaves blowing in the wind, washing blowing on the line, wind moving branches, butterflies and other insects flying and fluttering.

Objects with regular movement:

- Sand pictures (the sand is inside a frame and moves slowly from top to bottom, making new patterns as the picture is turned around);
- fluid pictures (the same as sand pictures, but using coloured fluid);

- large egg-timers;
- any toys that have a distinctive movement, such as 'nodding dogs', butterflies with flapping wings, and so on;
- 'executive' toys that have movement, for example Newton's cradle, a popular toy of the 1970s, which worked on perpetual motion;
- bubble tubes: mains-operated Perspex tubes that come in different sizes, and have bubbles inside that change colour;
- fascination tubes: small liquid-filled tubes with a bubble inside, which rises to the top of the tubes — turn them over and the bubble starts rising again;
- 'oil-lamps': these contain oil bubbles which make changing patterns as they move up and down (also popular in the 1970s);
- gyroscopes.

Note: Many of these objects can be bought in art, gift or curio shops, or through educational catalogues. A good example of the latter is TFH. You will find their address in Appendix III.

LOOKING AT OBJECTS ACTIVITIES
Sound

What to do

1. Sit or lay the child down, making sure you are both comfortable.

2. Shake or twirl the wind-chimes to attract the child's attention and keep her interest.

3. If the chimes are hanging up, point to them and see if she can follow your finger.

4. Hold her near to the chimes and encourage her to touch them or reach towards them.

5. Chat while you play and talk about what the chimes are doing.

Variations

◆ Twirl the wind-chimes near to your face.

◆ Move the wind-chimes nearer to or further away from the child.

◆ Change their position so that the child has to look up, straight ahead or to the side.

◆ You can darken the room and shine a torch onto the chimes to catch the light.

◆ Try varying the background: for example, a plain white wall, a coloured sheet, a pattern, a mirror.

◆ Leave the child alone to explore the toy — you could fix up a wind source, such as an open window or a *safe* portable fan, to keep the chimes moving.

Similar activities

You can carry out similar activities with different kinds of equipment. For example:

◆ bells;

◆ balloons with bells inside;

◆ balls with bells or stones inside;

◆ pom-poms (such as cheerleaders use — these rustle as they are shaken);

◆ home-made toys and mobiles: for example, hang fir cones on strings so that they will knock together in the breeze, perhaps spraying them with gold or silver paint first;

You will need:

a set of wind-chimes, either hung where the child can easily see them, or held in your hand.

Useful words and phrases:

look; up there; what is it?; can you see the chimes?; can you hear the chimes?; here they go; isn't it pretty?; it's blowing.

- natural environmental effects, for example falling leaves, falling rain or snow, leaves blowing in the wind, rustling branches;
- 'executive' toys that have sound and movement, for example Newton's cradle, a popular toy of the 1970s, which worked on perpetual motion;
- squeezy toys;
- activity centres;
- clockwork or battery toys that make a noise: for example, chattering teeth, toy soldiers, barking dogs, grunting pigs and so on;
- rattles and other sound-making toys;
- toys with sound effects, such as guns, spaceships, cars, teddies with 'growlers', and so on.

LOOKING AT OBJECTS
ACTIVITIES
Colour

What to do

1 Sit or lay the child down.

2 Sit or stand opposite her and wave the streamers around in the air, gently at first, then more energetically.

3 Chat to the child while you play and talk about what you are doing.

Variations

◆ Move the streamers around so that they are nearer to or further away from the child.

◆ Change their position so that she has to look up, straight ahead or to the side.

◆ Try varying the background: for example, a plain white wall, a coloured sheet, a pattern, a mirror.

◆ Vary the colours: for example, you could have a whole block of red streamers, then yellow ones, and so on.

◆ You could sprinkle glitter on the streamers or spray them gold or silver, to make them even more eye-catching.

Similar activities

You can carry out similar activities with different kinds of equipment. For example:
◆ mobiles;
◆ colourful chimes;
◆ colourful spinning tops;
◆ sparklers;
◆ outdoor fireworks;
◆ colourful 'executive' toys;
◆ computer programmes showing colours and patterns;
◆ slide shows and projected patterns (you can show these on a cine-screen or a plain white wall);
◆ colourful lights;
◆ kaleidoscopes;
◆ 'bug-eye' (an instrument that multiplies what you are looking at, just like an insect's eye);
◆ all colourful toys and those with coloured lights.

(!) Please be careful with all electrical equipment.

You will need:

multicoloured streamers, which you can make from crepe paper or even cut out from glossy magazines.

Useful words and phrases:

look; here; what is it?; look at the pretty colours; it's going up ... and down; names of colours.

What to do

You will need:

a torch, preferably one that has different colours.

Useful words and phrases:

look; there; what is it?; can you see the light?; look at the pretty colours; it's flashing; names of colours; torch.

1 Sit or lie down with the child, making sure you are both comfortable.

2 Shine the torch onto a suitable blank wall a short way from the child, where she can easily see it.

3 Move the torch around so that the light makes patterns on the wall.

4 Gradually darken the room to get the best effect. (This must be done at the child's own pace and may take a few minutes or several weeks, depending on the child.)

5 Point to the light and see if the child can follow your finger.

6 Chat to her while you play and talk about what you are doing.

Variations

◆ Move the torch around so that the light is nearer to or further away from the child.

◆ Change the position of the light so that she has to look up, straight ahead or to the side.

◆ Try varying the background: for example, a plain white wall, a coloured sheet, a pattern, a mirror.

◆ Shine the torch onto mobiles, moving toys, your own face, and so on.

◆ Change the colour of the light.

◆ If you only have a plain torch, you can fix coloured paper or Perspex in front of the torch to change the colour.

◆ Flash the torch on and off; speed it up or slow it down; or make a sequence.

Similar activities

You can carry out similar activities with different kinds of equipment. For example:

- Christmas lights (fairy lights);
- mirrors (flash them to catch the light, or shine a torch onto them);
- refraction paper and mirrors;
- hologram pictures;
- laser discs;
- kaleidoscopes;
- shadow pictures;
- candles (may also be coloured and/or scented);
- sparklers;
- indoor fireworks;
- outdoor fireworks;
- bubble tubes;
- fibre-optic lights (very popular in the 1960s);
- fluid pictures;
- slide shows and projected patterns (you can show these on a cine-screen or a plain white wall);
- toys with lights: for example, spinning tops, yo-yos, cars, guns and 'laser beams' (as popularized by the film *Star Wars*), which light up when used;
- Pethna Box: this is a 'plug-in' activity centre with lights, air and music, made by TFH (see Appendix III for address).

Note: Many of these objects can be bought in art, gift or curio shops, or through educational catalogues.

Please be careful with all electrical equipment. Do not shine lights directly into children's eyes, unless cleared to do so by a specialist in visual impairment.

Take special care, when using darkened rooms, flashing lights and similar effects, with children who have epilepsy or visual sensitivity, as overstimulation may bring on an epileptic attack or migraine.

You will need:

a glove puppet, preferably something fairly big and eye-catching.

Useful words and phrases:

here's (name of puppet)!; he says hello; oops, he's gone; where's he gone?; bye-bye puppet; here he is; back again; say hello.

What to do

1 You can do this anywhere, even on a bus, if you don't mind people looking at you.

2 Put on the puppet and play around with it, making it say hello, do a little dance or whatever captures the child's attention and entertains her.

3 Let her touch and feel it if she wants to.

4 Hide the puppet behind your back, say, "Where's it gone?" and bring it back quickly while the child is still looking. Say, "Here it is!" with exaggerated surprise.

5 Do this several times, making a big fuss each time the puppet disappears and reappears.

6 If you lose the child's attention, go back to step 3 and see if you can recapture it. If not, either try a variation or change to another game.

7 Try to end the game before she gets bored, and let her play with the puppet, or do a little 'show' for her.

Variations

◆ Move around with the puppet before hiding him.

◆ Hide the puppet under the child's leg or foot, or behind her back.

◆ Hide the puppet under her clothes.

◆ Make the puppet go behind furniture or under the table, but don't hide it for too long, or the child will stop looking.

◆ Try the same game with different toys — especially soft animals, teddies or large dolls.

Similar activities

You can carry out similar activities with different toys. For example:

- hide a sweet or very small toy under your hand (don't hide it too many times, especially a sweet, as the child is sure to want it and will get frustrated if you tease her);
- try magic tricks, where objects just disappear and reappear as if by magic from some unlikely place;
- post objects into a box, so that they come straight out again: you can buy toys that produce this effect, or make one from a cardboard box, cutting holes in both ends;
- put toys on the table and cover them with a cloth or box lid, but do not leave them covered for long, as the idea is to keep the child's attention;
- try out different toys where things disappear and reappear immediately, such as toys where you hammer pegs or balls into holes, or helter-skelters, where a marble goes round and round in a 'now you see it, now you don't' fashion.

Please be careful of small toys that the child could put into her mouth and which could make her choke. As you will want to reward her good attention by letting her play with the toys, or eat the sweets, make sure they are suitable.

© *Jackie Cooke 1996*
You may photocopy this page for instructional use only

LOOKING AT OBJECTS ACTIVITIES
Anticipation

You will need:

a Jack-in-the-box.

Useful words and phrases:

box; here's Jack!; he says hello; oops, he's gone; where's he gone?; bye-bye, Jack; here he is; back again; say hello; up he pops.

What to do

1 You can do this anywhere, even on a bus, if you don't mind people looking at you.

2 If the child is on the nervous side, it is best to show her Jack out of the box first, and have a little chat or game with him. Let her touch and feel him if she wants to.

3 Play around, making Jack say hello, to capture the child's attention and entertain her.

4 When you have her complete attention, press Jack's lid down so that he disappears, and say, "Where's he gone?" Make him reappear quickly while she is still looking for him. Say, "Here he is!", with exaggerated surprise.

5 Do this several times, making a big fuss each time Jack disappears and reappears.

6 If you lose the child's attention, go back to step 3 and see if you can recapture it. If not, either try a variation or change to another game.

7 Try to end the game before she gets bored, and let her play with the toy.

32

Early Sensory Skills

Variations

◆ You can either stay on the same side as the child, so that she can only see the toy, or sit by the toy so that she can see you both.

◆ You can cut out most of the speech, and just say, "Look".

◆ Help the child push Jack back into his box.

◆ Help her to press the button or lever which makes Jack jump out again.

◆ Take turns to make Jack appear or disappear.

Similar activities

You can carry out similar activities with different toys. You do not always need elaborate shop-bought toys — the main point is the element of surprise, which creates anticipation and keeps the child looking. For example:

◆ build up and knock down bricks;

◆ bubbles;

◆ balloons, especially if you let them go as soon as you've blown them up (some also make a squeaking or whistling noise as they deflate);

◆ party blowers, especially the ones with a feather in the end;

◆ pop-up books;

◆ there are all sorts of action toys available from toyshops that do something when you operate them.

LOOKING AT OBJECTS ACTIVITIES
Tracking (Side to Side)

You will need:

a medium-sized, eye-catching ball; a table or large tray (optional).

Useful words and phrases:

ball; look; there it goes; here it comes; it's getting closer; roll the ball.

What to do

1 The child can sit at a table or on the floor for this game.

2 Show her the ball and have a little game or chat about it.

3 Sit opposite her and simply roll the ball in front of the child, across her line of vision, trying to keep it in her sight. Start by rolling it from her left to her right. Talk about what you are doing. (If you use a tray, you will not have to pick up the ball, or lean to get it so often, as it will not roll far. A tray also limits the distance the child has to look at, so it may be useful for children with narrow fields of vision.)

4 Roll the ball back the other way.

5 Do this several times, making a big fuss each time the ball is directly in front of the child.

6 If you lose her attention, go back to step 2 and see if you can recapture it. If not, either try a variation or change to another game.

7 Try to end the game before she gets bored, and let her play with the ball, or have a little game together.

Variations

◆ Try a ball with a bell or other sound-making toy inside — a noise can often help to attract and keep a child's attention for a longer period.

◆ Decorate the ball with glitter or silver stars if it is not eye-catching enough, but make sure it can still roll smoothly.

◆ Gently throw the ball from side to side.

◆ Sit the same side as the child.

◆ Once the child is tracking a slow ball you can speed it up.

◆ Once she is tracking the ball backwards and forwards once, you can roll it several times in a row.

Similar activities

You can carry out similar activities with different kinds of equipment. For example:

◆ toys on strings;
◆ toy cars and other vehicles;
◆ wheeled toys, such as horses, brick carts and so on;
◆ clockwork toys (as long as they go in a reasonably straight line);
◆ blowing bubbles (along, not up);
◆ roll out a party streamer or Christmas garland and, if possible, reel it back in again;
◆ balloons (side to side only);
◆ make your hand or fingers 'walk' in front of the child;
◆ move toys, shiny paper and so on across the child's line of vision;
◆ an accordion (move one side only);
◆ paint a large, colourful brush stroke across paper;
◆ use computer-based tracking programmes.

What to do

1 The child can sit at a table or on the floor for this game.

2 Sit opposite her and drop the yo-yo down once; catch it and show it to her.

3 Do this several times, making a big fuss each time the yo-yo comes back up.

4 If you lose her attention, try a variation or change to another game.

5 Try to end the game before she gets bored, and let her play with the yo-yo if it is safe.

Variations

◆ Try a yo-yo that makes a noise.

◆ Decorate the yo-yo with glitter or silver stars if it is not eye-catching enough.

◆ Sit the same side as the child.

◆ Once she can track the yo-yo up and down once, you can do it several times in a row.

◆ If the yo-yo has a light, play the game in the dark or half-dark.

Similar activities

You can carry out similar activities with different kinds of equipment. For example:

◆ toys on elastic;

◆ bounce or throw a ball up and down;

◆ bubbles (blow them up into the air);

◆ balloons (up and down only);

◆ bouncing toys;

◆ toys on springs (but take care of the eyes — yours and the child's);

◆ make your hand or fingers 'climb' up and down in front of the child;

◆ move toys, shiny paper and so on up and down;

◆ paint a large, colourful brush stroke up and down paper;

◆ use computer-based tracking programmes.

You will need:

a yo-yo, preferably with a light inside.

Useful words and phrases:

yo-yo; look; there it goes; here it comes; it's getting closer; up and down.

LOOKING AT OBJECTS ACTIVITIES
Books

What to do

1 You can do this anywhere, but quiet, relaxed surroundings, where you can spend some time together, are probably the best.

2 Sit beside the child or have her on your lap.

3 Open the book and show her the pictures, introducing Spot the dog.

4 Tell the story, in as interesting a way as possible. Don't be afraid to go 'over the top', as young children like this.

5 When you come to the flaps, exaggerate the excitement: for example, "Is Spot in here? *No*! Where *can* he be?", and so on. Encourage the child to lift the flaps if she can.

6 Let the child set the pace — if she wants to ask questions, or to linger over a picture, you must respond.

7 Read the story as many times as she wants you to (and you can stand), but try to finish before she gets bored.

Variations

◆ There are not many formal variations: the variations are in the way you tell the story — how much expression you use, how much the child is involved, and so on.

◆ You can make a little game out of it by introducing soft toys at each appropriate point. It is probably easiest to stick to Spot, bringing him out at the end when he is found, and have him 'chase' the child, and so on.

◆ You could act out the story with soft toys, puppets or plastic animals after you have read the book.

Similar activities

You can carry out similar activities with different kinds of books. For example:

◆ pop-up books;

◆ books with lift-out parts or sticky pictures that can be moved around;

◆ books with other mechanisms, such as sound effects, squeakers, buzzers, pull-outs and tabs, press buttons, and so on;

◆ books with accompanying tapes.

You will need:

"Where's Spot?"
lift-the-flap book.

Useful words and phrases:

book; story; Spot;
turn the page;
lift the flap; where's Spot?;
is he here?;
no, it's [name of character];
Mummy; Spot's mummy;
here he is; at last; finished.

Looking at Objects
CHECKLIST

Child's name	

Date	Activity		Comments/Responses
	Looking at Objects	Movement	
		Sound	
		Colour	
		Light and Dark	
		Hiding Games	
		Anticipation	
		Tracking (side to side)	
		Tracking (up and down)	
		Books	
		Child's Preferred Toys	

TOUCH

SECTION 2

INTRODUCTION

THIS SECTION is about the sense of touch and is divided into two parts: 'Tactile Awareness' and 'Tactile Exploration'. Most of the activities are better suited for one-to-one work. This is especially true for very young children, or for those with physical handicaps or learning difficulties, who need a lot of help and attention.

It is hoped that the child will eventually begin to explore the materials actively and not just respond to them. This is the time to encourage the kinds of exploration activities described in the second part of this section. You should now give any help that is necessary, including guiding the child's hands. However only use physical guidance to help the child, not to do the activity for her.

Aims

1 To stimulate the child.

2 To raise the child's awareness of her sense of touch.

3 To encourage interactions between the child and her carer.

4 To encourage communication between the child and her carer.

5 To build up the child's concepts about objects.

6 To teach the child appropriate vocabulary.

Hints

If you are working with groups of children you will need vast quantities of some of the materials used, as you will have to throw away any that get wet, dirty or go into the child's mouth. On the positive side, many of the materials are cheap to buy, or can be found in ordinary households, or as offcuts and left-overs from industry, so it pays to ask around.

If you work in a school or nursery, keep materials in a variety of containers such as large jars, trays and large bags, for convenience and flexibility.

Take Care

In today's climate, allegations of sexual abuse are a very real issue for people working with young children. Take all precautions necessary to ensure that your activities cannot be misinterpreted. In schools and nurseries it may be unwise to carry out some of the touching games and activities described in the manual when working alone with a child. Male staff must take particular care. Always follow the guidelines of the establishment you are working in.

TACTILE AWARENESS

The emphasis here is on the child experiencing different kinds of touch, ranging from air wafting on her face to being tickled. She may be unable to do much for herself at this stage, in which case the adult will do most of the actions. However, the child will enjoy the activities and at the same time they will stimulate her senses, help her to make a relationship with her helper and provide a simple form of play.

Alternatively, the child may be at a more active stage, and attempt to explore the materials, to make choices about what to play with and to communicate. We hope that all children will progress from being a passive participant to being an active one, and go on to the exploratory activities described in the next part.

You can also use these activities with older or more able children, in order to teach them the appropriate vocabulary. Use the activities as quick, 'fun' games or adapt them for 'science' experiments.

Additional aims

1 To teach the child about her body and help develop body image.

2 To arouse the child's interest in the person or object causing the sensation.

3 To encourage eye-contact between the child and her carer.

4 To arouse the child's interest in active exploration.

5 To give the child opportunities to express her preferences, by accepting or refusing activities.

TACTILE AWARENESS ACTIVITIES
Air

You will need:

fans, such as Spanish or Chinese fans; or make your own from thick paper or card.

Useful words and phrases:

air; blow; feel; cool; warm; more.

What to do

1. Sit or lay the child down, but make sure you are both comfortable.

2. Fan her hands, fairly gently and not too close at first, so that she does not get scared.

3. Look for any of these responses, either to the fan, or to you: smiling; looking; turning towards or away from the air; pushing away; pulling your hand or the fan nearer; taking the fan; fanning herself; fanning you; asking for more, or for the fan. These responses may show like or dislike, or simply mean 'not at the moment'. It is important to respect the child's choices and respond appropriately to them.

Variations

◆ Vary the speed.

◆ Hold the fan nearer or further away from the child.

◆ Pause for a while, or stop fanning, to see her reaction.

◆ Fan other parts of the child's body, but start gently with each new area.

Similar activities

You can carry out similar activities with different kinds of equipment. For example:

◆ battery-operated mini-fans;
◆ electric household fans (various sizes and strengths);
◆ balloons;
◆ bellows;
◆ hairdryers (on low heat);
◆ pumps (for blowing up balloons, air-beds, bicycle tyres and so on);
◆ your own breath (but be hygienic);
◆ Pethna Box: this is a 'plug-in' activity centre, made by TFH (see p 165 for address). You have a number of options: *you* can control the toy, it can be set on automatic, or the child can operate it herself, using a variety of simple switches. It produces air, music and flashing lights, together or separately.

Please be careful whenever you blow air at a child, especially onto her face. Check the power on yourself first!

TACTILE AWARENESS ACTIVITIES
Spraying

You will need:

a plant-sprayer, with the nozzle turned to spray; a towel.

Useful words and phrases:

water; wet; dry; warm; cool; cold; spray; towel.

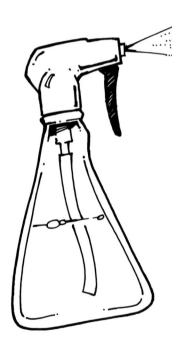

What to do

1 This activity can be done with the child sitting or lying down, or as part of a 'rough-and-tumble' game. You must be somewhere warm, as she is going to get wet.

2 If this is done as a sensory experience, be gentle.

3 Always talk to the child and tell her what you are doing and about to do.

4 Start with warm, but not hot, water, and spray a little directly onto her hand. Hold the sprayer far enough away for the water spray to be as soft as possible.

5 Look for any of these responses: smiling; laughing; crying; pulling her hand away; pushing you or the spray away; holding out her hand so that you can spray it again. These responses may show like or dislike, or simply mean 'not at the moment'. It is important to respect the child's choices and respond appropriately to them. For example, if she continues to push the sprayer away, stop the activity.

6 Dry the child thoroughly afterwards.

Variations

◆ Hold the spray nearer to or further away from the child.

◆ Vary the amount of water in one spray.

◆ Change the speed and concentration of water, from spray to jet.

◆ Vary the temperature of the water, within reason.

◆ Spray other parts of the child's body— face, back, feet, and so on, but always start gently with each new area. *Be especially careful of the face and eyes.* (However, strange as it may seem, some children love being sprayed directly in the face, and responses such as screwing up the face and shutting the eyes can mean anticipation and delight.)

◆ Move the sprayer around to different angles to see if she turns towards or away from it.

◆ Pause for a while, to see how she responds.

◆ Build up her suspense and see if she shows anticipation.

Similar activities

You can carry out similar activities with different kinds of equipment. For example:

◆ coloured water;
◆ bubbly or soapy water;
◆ bubbles;
◆ water scented with, for example, bubble bath or oil;
◆ scent, perfume, toilet water, after-shave sprays;
◆ watering-can.

 Please do not spray the child's face with anything other than ordinary water, as some substances can irritate. Always avoid the eyes.

TACTILE AWARENESS ACTIVITIES
Splashing & Plunging

You will need:

a bowl of warm water; towel; apron (optional).

Useful words and phrases:

water; wet; dry; warm; cool; cold; splash; in; bowl.

What to do

1 Put an apron or overall on the child, as she will get wet.

2 She should sit or stand where she can easily plunge her hands into the bowl of water, but not knock it over.

3 Be gentle and non-threatening.

4 Always chat to the child and tell her what you are doing or going to do.

5 Start with warm, but not hot, water and place one of her hands on top of the water. As she gets used to it, gently trickle water onto her hand, then gradually put it right into the water.

6 Put both her hands in the water, and encourage her to splash and move them around.

7 Look for any responses that may indicate like or dislike, wanting more of the activity, or wanting to finish it. These include: smiling; laughing; crying; grimacing; pulling her hands away from the water; moving her hands spontaneously in the water; and so on. Respect her choices and respond appropriately to them.

8 Dry the child off thoroughly afterwards.

Variations

◆ Vary the temperature of the water, within reason.

◆ Help the child move her hands: slowly, quickly, gently, vigorously, and so on.

◆ Put her feet in the water.

Similar activities

You can carry out similar activities with different kinds of equipment. For example:

◆ coloured water;

◆ bubbly or soapy water;

◆ water scented and softened with bath-oil, foam or bathcubes;

- an ordinary water-play tray (as found in any nursery);
- foot spa (this vibrates the water and is very relaxing; it runs off the mains and can be bought from major stores);
- paddling pool;
- put toys or objects that encourage simple hand movements in the water, such as jugs, ducks and boats;
- put the water in different-shaped containers, such as a jelly-mould;
- use see-through and non-see-through bowls.

 Please make sure that these activities take place in a warm environment.

TACTILE AWARENESS ACTIVITIES
Brushing & Stroking

You will need:

a large, soft, thick-bristled make-up brush, of the type that can be bought in make-up departments of large stores.

Useful words and phrases:

brush; soft; hard; gentle; stiff; tickle; brushing.

What to do

1 The child can sit up or lie down for this activity, but make sure you are both comfortable, as it is meant to be fairly relaxing.

2 Be gentle and non-threatening.

3 Always talk to the child, telling her what you are doing or about to do.

4 Gently brush the back of her hand, which is usually less sensitive than the palm.

5 When she has got used to the sensation, brush the palm of her hand, each finger separately, and in between the fingers.

6 Look for responses that may show like or dislike, or 'not at the moment'. These include: smiling; laughing; crying; holding out her hand for more; pulling her hand away; turning her hand over; pushing you or the brush away; knocking the brush from your hand; pulling your hand or the brush nearer; and so on. Respect her choices and respond appropriately.

Variations

◆ Brush faster and slower.

◆ Use different amounts of pressure.

◆ Vary the type of brushes you use: from thick to thin, from very soft to fairly stiff, from large to small; for example, make-up brushes, paint-brushes, paste or glue brushes.

◆ Brush other parts of the child's body, especially the back of her neck, legs, feet, back and arms, but start gently with each new area.

(!) **Do not use very stiff brushes such as floor-brushes, which might hurt. Always make sure your equipment is clean!**

Similar activities

You can carry out similar activities with different kinds of equipment. For example:

- ◆ feathers;
- ◆ feather dusters;
- ◆ tissues;
- ◆ cotton wool;
- ◆ cotton wool buds;
- ◆ soft sponges;
- ◆ talcum-powder puffs;
- ◆ soft leaves;
- ◆ silky scarves;
- ◆ your own fingers, gently stroking or tickling;
- ◆ hair-brush — gently brush the child's hair.

(!) Make sure everything is clean and be aware of allergies. It is best not to use feathers on or near the face.

TACTILE AWARENESS ACTIVITIES
Light Materials

You will need:

a scrap of silk, for example from a scarf.

Useful words and phrases:

silk; soft; gentle; stroke; light.

What to do

1 Sit or lay the child down, but make sure you are both comfortable, as this is meant to be fairly relaxing.

2 Be gentle and non-threatening.

3 Always talk to the child, telling her what you are doing or about to do.

4 Place the silk on the back of her hand, or let it float down onto it.

5 Gently stroke her hand with the silk.

6 Place it in the palm of her hand.

7 Look for responses showing like or dislike, or meaning 'not now'. These include: smiling; laughing; crying; shaking her head; throwing the silk on the floor; reaching for it. Respect the child's choices and respond appropriately.

Variations

◆ Vary the speed of stroking.
◆ Use a variety of touch — firm, gentle, tickling.
◆ Wind the silk gently around the child's hands.
◆ Place the silk on different parts of her face and body.
◆ Blow it gently at her face.
◆ Put it on top of her head.

Similar activities

You can carry out similar activities with different materials. Collect them from old clothes and around the house, wash them thoroughly and store them in a box. For example:
◆ tissues;
◆ tissue paper;
◆ nylon;
◆ scraps cut from old tights or stockings;
◆ light scarves, especially ones that have shiny or glittery weaves, to catch the child's eye;
◆ light woollen scarves;

- cotton;
- satin;
- velvet;
- shawls;
- you can also hold materials up to the light to look through.

Be careful when putting material over the head and face, especially large pieces. Make sure the child can breathe properly and does not get the material tangled around her neck. Beware, too, of material with decorations such as sequins and small beads, as they could be swallowed or irritate the skin.

TACTILE AWARENESS ACTIVITIES
Vibration

You will need:

Vibrobubble (available from TFH — see p 165 for address): this is a battery-run ball, which vibrates when you put your hands on the pressure points.

Useful words and phrases:

Vibrobubble; touch; vibrate; hands; more?; finished?

What to do

1 The child can sit or lie down, but make sure she is in a comfortable position to feel and operate the bubble.

2 Place her hands on the pressure points. The vibration should start automatically.

3 Leave her hands on the vibrobubble. If she takes them off, wait a little while, then put them back. (However, if she keeps removing them, take the toy away.)

4 Look for responses showing like or dislike or meaning 'not now'. These include: smiling; laughing; crying; shaking her head; removing her hands purposefully; keeping her hands on the bubble; voluntarily returning her hands to the bubble. Respect the child's choices and respond appropriately.

Variations

◆ Let the child feel the vibration with other parts of her body — cheeks, feet, lips and so on.

◆ Cover the bubble with different materials, so that the child can feel them as she feels the vibration; for example, use fur, sheepskin, velvet, silk, suede, wool and chiffon.

Similar activities

You can carry out similar activities with a variety of equipment. Some of these items are ordinary household appliances, while others are made specifically for this activity. For example:

◆ washing machine;
◆ vacuum cleaner;
◆ tumble dryer;
◆ fridge (if yours vibrates);
◆ vibration tubes: available from TFH (see p 165 for address);
◆ electric massagers: you can buy these from high street stores;
◆ drum;
◆ tuning fork (hold it near the child's ear);
◆ vibrating cushion (for use with the Pethna Box: the child sits on it and it acts as a switch to operate the Pethna Box — see p 45 for a description);
◆ water bed/vibrating bed;
◆ foot spa: this can be bought from many high street stores.

! An advantage of some vibrating toys and activities is that they do not need much adult intervention, so the child can quite happily play by herself for a while. *But keep your eye on the child and the equipment at all times.*

Remember: *never* encourage children to get inside any household appliance, or to put their hands inside. They should only feel the vibration from the outside.

TACTILE AWARENESS ACTIVITIES
Textured Surfaces

You will need:

a textured lap tray (some of these trays come with a built-in cushion, which is comfortable to have on the lap, and so are especially useful for children who cannot move around much).

Useful words and phrases:

touch; feel; soft; hard; tray; hands; feet.

What to do

1 The child should be sitting up (at a table if you prefer, but this is not necessary).

2 Place the tray on her lap (or the table) and put her hands on top of it, palms down.

3 Encourage her to feel the texture by patting or moving her hands over the tray.

4 Always talk to her, telling her what you are doing or going to do.

5 Look for any responses that show like or dislike, wanting more or wanting to finish. These include: smiling; laughing; crying; keeping her hands on the tray; pulling her hands away; voluntarily returning her hands to the tray. Respect the child's choices and respond appropriately.

Variations

◆ Place the child's feet on the tray.

◆ Let the child put her face on the tray.

◆ Put her knees and elbows on the tray.

◆ If you cannot find a textured tray, stick different materials onto an ordinary one.

Similar activities

You can carry out similar activities with almost any kind of surface. For a child who has to spend a lot of time sitting down, having different textured lap trays or textures fixed to a chair-tray would make an interesting change as a tactile activity in its own right, or to provide a changing surface for other activities.

When deciding on the surfaces, think of different textures, temperatures and how pleasant they are to touch. Textured objects can also be fixed to the table for the child to feel eg.

◆ wood;

◆ brick;

◆ materials, such as fur, velvet, suede, cotton;

◆ smooth surfaces, such as melamine, plastic;

◆ rough surfaces, such as kitchen scourers, sandpaper;

◆ raised-pattern or flock wallpaper;

◆ packaging material, such as foam, polystyrene;

◆ different surfaces for the child to sit or lie upon, such as a sheepskin rug, a rubber mat.

TACTILE AWARENESS ACTIVITIES
Sticky Textures

What to do

1 Remove the jelly from the fridge a little while before it is wanted, so that it is not too cold.

2 Put a small amount of jelly on the child's hand. As she gets used to it, put on more.

3 Place her hands on top of the jelly.

4 If she likes it, put her hands into the bowl of jelly.

5 Always talk to her, telling her what you are doing or going to do.

6 Look for responses showing like or dislike, or meaning 'not now'. These include: smiling; laughing; crying; shaking her head; removing her hands purposefully; keeping her hands in the jelly; voluntarily returning her hands to the jelly; shaking her hands to get rid of the jelly. Respect the child's choices and respond appropriately.

7 Wash and dry her hands afterwards.

Variations

◆ It does not matter if the child eats some jelly, as no-one else can use it; make sure her hands are clean first.

◆ Put jelly on other parts of her body — lips, elbows, feet, and so on (but not to be eaten afterwards!).

◆ Use half-set jelly.

◆ Use cubes of raw jelly.

Similar activities

You can carry out similar activities with lots of sticky substances, as long as they can be pulled about. *Some of these must not go into the mouth.* For example:

Things you cannot eat:
◆ paint,
◆ Soft Stuff,
◆ Playdoh,

You will need:

a bowl of ordinary jelly, any flavour, made up and set.

Useful words and phrases:

jelly; sticky; feel; taste; names of colours; names of flavours.

57

- putty,
- clay,
- plasticine,
- Blu-Tack or Hold-it
- Slime: the trade name of a substance you can buy from joke shops,
- wet sand,
- wet flour.

Things you can eat:
- dough,
- cake mixture,
- marmalade,
- wet cooked rice,
- cold cooked pasta.

Never mix the things you can and cannot eat in one session, or even in one day. Use different types of container to emphasize the difference: for example, 'working' trays for the non-edible substances, and ordinary plates and bowls for the edible ones. You do not want to teach the child that it is all right to put everything into her mouth.

TACTILE AWARENESS ACTIVITIES
Dry Textures

What to do

1 The child should be seated comfortably at the table.

2 Put the empty tray in front of her. You may need to fix it so that it does not slip around on the table. A non-slip mat, Blu-Tack or Hold-it can be used.

3 Pour the rice slowly into the tray, pausing occasionally. This is so the child can look and listen to the sound and anticipate more rice coming. Only put in a small amount at first.

4 Place one of the child's hands on top of the rice.

5 Gently move her hand on the rice.

6 As she gets used to it, put her other hand in the tray, and move both hands around.

7 Always talk to her, telling her what you are doing or going to do.

8 Look for any responses that may show like or dislike, wanting more or wanting to finish the activity. These include: smiling; laughing; crying; keeping her hands in the tray; pulling her hands away; voluntarily returning her hands to the tray. Respect the child's choices and respond appropriately.

Variations

◆ Vary the amount of rice in the tray.

◆ Pour rice gently over the child's hands.

◆ Vary the speed and amount of rice you pour on her hands.

◆ Bury her hands in the rice.

◆ Put other parts of her body in the tray of rice — feet, arms, legs, but not her face.

◆ Shake the tray about, gently at first, so she can feel the rice moving against her hands or feet.

! **Do not allow the child to eat the rice.**

You will need:

a bag of dry rice; a tray with sides that are deep enough to keep the rice inside, but shallow enough for the child to put her hands in with ease. (Cat-litter trays are actually a good size, but only use new ones!)

Useful words and phrases:

rice; tray; feel; tickle; shake; listen; look.

Similar activities

Instead of using a tray, some substances can be put into big bags, so that the child's hands or feet can be plunged inside. Ordinary paper or plastic bags can be used, although you could buy or make cloth bags, which are stronger and last longer.

You can carry out similar activities with a wide range of substances, most of which can be found around the house, and are fairly cheap to buy. Keep them in separate jars and they can be used over and over again. For example:

- different kinds of sand, from very fine to fairly coarse;
- flour;
- cornflour;
- dried peas, beans* and lentils;
- dried pasta shapes and spaghetti;
- clean, unused straw;
- clean, unused wood shavings;
- clean packaging material;
- fir cones and dried leaves.

 Do not let the child eat dried foods or put them in her nose or ears. Supervise the child closely at all times.

__Never__ use red kidney beans as they are poisonous before soaking and cooking.

TACTILE AWARENESS ACTIVITIES
Massage & Firm Touch

What to do

1 The child can sit or lie down. Make sure both of you are comfortable, as this is meant to be a fairly relaxing activity.

2 Sprinkle a little talc onto the back of one of the child's hands, which is usually less sensitive than the palm.

3 Rub the talc in gently, with one finger.

4 Sprinkle on more talc and rub her whole hand. Put talc on her palm and gently rub her palm and each finger separately.

5 Always talk to the child, telling her what you are doing or going to do.

6 Look for any responses that may show like or dislike, wanting more, or wanting to finish. These include: smiling; laughing; crying; holding out her hand for more; pulling her hand away; pushing your hand away. Respect the child's choices and respond appropriately.

Variations

◆ Vary your pressure when massaging the talc into the child's hands.

◆ Vary the speed.

◆ Use more or less talc.

◆ Let her smell the talc.

◆ Sprinkle the talc in the air to encourage the child to look (but not too much, as you could both end up sneezing!).

◆ Put talc on different parts of her body — feet, tummy, back — but not the face. Always start by just sprinkling it, and then massaging if she likes it.

◆ Sprinkle a little talc onto your hand or the child's and blow it off.

 Do not use talc too near the face as it could be inhaled.

Talc may be harmful to children with asthma and other respiratory conditions, so it would be best to avoid using it with them.

You will need:

talcum powder (use unperfumed if the child has any allergy to scented products); apron (optional: this can become a messy activity).

Useful words and phrases:

talc; soft; touch; rub; massage; smell.

Some children may find having their hands held and massaged too intrusive at first, but might be less sensitive on other parts of their body.

Similar activities

You can carry out similar activities with a wide range of equipment. For example:

Suitable for the face:
◆ make-up;
◆ face paints;
◆ lip balm, chapstick and so on;
◆ facial creams and moisturizers;
◆ diluted essential oils, as used in aromatherapy (available from many high street shops).

Not suitable for the face:
◆ hand cream;
◆ shaving foam;
◆ hair gel;
◆ hair mousse;
◆ baby oil;
◆ massage oils (except diluted essential oils);
◆ wooden massager (available from high street shops);
◆ Japanese balls (also available from high street shops; they are used to rub or massage the back, the feet and so on).

Check whether the child has allergies. You can buy non-perfumed, non-allergenic goods.
Always consult a doctor and/or physiotherapist if there is any doubt whatsoever over the suitability of using massage with a particular child.

You should be suitably trained and/or experienced if planning a genuine massage, especially if using essential oils.

TACTILE AWARENESS ACTIVITIES

Finger Rhymes & Tickle Games

What to do

1 The child can sit or lie down for this activity.

2 Be gentle and unthreatening.

3 Sit face-to-face or beside the child, and take her hand gently, holding it palm upwards.

4 Always talk to her, telling her what you are doing or going to do.

5 Sing 'Walkie Round the Garden' as you tickle her hand. Here is the whole rhyme with actions:

Walkie round the Garden
Like a Teddy Bear, (Tickle the child's palm softly)

One step,
Two steps ('Walk' up her arm)

And tickly under there. (Tickle her under the arm)

6 Look for any responses that show like or dislike, wanting more or wanting to finish the activity. These include: smiling; laughing; crying; pulling her hands away. Respect the child's choices and respond appropriately.

Variations

◆ End up by tickling the child under the chin, or behind her ear, or on the back of her neck, or her tummy.

◆ Start with the sole of her foot, instead of her hand.

◆ Build up her anticipation by leaving a pause before the final word.

Similar activities

You can carry out similar activities with different songs and rhymes, or make up your own. For example:

◆ 'This Little Piggy went to Market' (usually tickling the toes and foot, but it can also be done on the hand);

You will need:

a knowledge of rhymes and tickle games, or a good book that tells you how to do them!

Useful words and phrases:

tickle; hand; ticklish; more?; again.

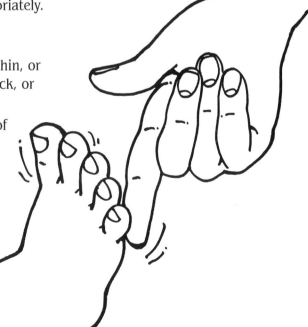

63

- 'Pat-a-Cake, Pat-a-Cake, Baker's Man' (clapping the child's hands with yours);
- 'One Finger, One Thumb, Keep Moving' (touching or stroking the child's finger and thumb, and so on);
- 'Shake My Hand' (shake the child's hand);
- tickling the child while building up her suspense verbally: for example, "I'm coming to get you … (pause), I'm going to tickle your … (pause) ear"; and so on.

(Please see Appendix II for the complete words.)

Tactile Awareness Activities
CHECKLIST

Child's name

Date	Activity		Comments/Responses
	Tactile Awareness	Air	
		Spraying	
		Splashing & Plunging	
		Brushing & Stroking	
		Light Materials	
		Vibration	
		Textured Surfaces	
		Sticky Textures	
		Dry Textures	
		Massage & Firm Touch	
		Finger Rhymes & Tickle Games	
		Child's Preferred Activities	

SECTION 2

© Jackie Cooke 1996
You may photocopy this page for instructional use only

65

Section 2: Touch

TACTILE EXPLORATION

The emphasis here is on the child actively exploring objects and materials in as many ways as she can. The helper can extend and develop what the child does by herself, and show her new ways to explore the toys. The helper should note the child's reactions to different activities and respond to her attempts to show preferences and make choices.

You can also use these activities with older or more able children, in order to teach them the appropriate vocabulary. Use the activities as quick, 'fun' games or adapt them for 'science' experiments.

Additional aims

1 To encourage the child to explore objects and materials with her hands and to develop different ways of doing so, to include:

- grasping,
- releasing,
- banging,
- waving,
- scratching,
- throwing and dropping,
- knocking over,
- squeezing,
- stretching,
- tearing,
- feeling carefully,
- using one hand,
- using both hands,
- picking up, with an increasingly sophisticated grip.

2 To give opportunities for the child to express preferences and to communicate choices about what she wants to do.

Remember!

- The child will need some mobility in her hands, so that she can actively explore.
- Let her explore by herself for a while, before you join in and show her new actions. If necessary, help her to get started by demonstrating what to do, putting her hands on the

object, or moving them around in the tray. If she rejects something, take it away.

◆ Always encourage her attempts to communicate.

◆ Try using the useful words.

◆ Respond to her choices and preferences, and respect her likes and dislikes.

◆ Do not make assumptions about the child's likes and dislikes — let her try things out.

◆ Be aware of possible allergies and sensitivity to equipment.

◆ Be aware of dangers, such as faulty equipment, passing germs, using small objects that may be swallowed, and so on.

◆ Be sensitive when using massage and touching activities involving the child's body. It may be wiser not to carry out these activities when you are alone with the child.

You will need:

a variety of silky materials;
a deep-sided tray (optional).

Useful words and phrases:

feel; silk; soft; silky.

What to do

1 Sit the child at a table so that she can comfortably reach the table or tray.

2 Put the materials on the table or in the tray.

3 Encourage the child to feel inside the tray (if applicable).

4 Sit back, and allow her to explore and feel the materials.

5 After a while you can join in, talk about the materials and show her different things to do with them. If necessary, guide her hands, so that she can explore as much as possible.

Variations

◆ Increase or decrease the number and variety of the materials.

◆ Encourage the child to carry out all sorts of actions, such as scrunching up the material, throwing it, blowing it, hiding under it, playing 'peep-bo', and so on.

Similar activities

You can carry out similar activities with a variety of materials, with or without a tray. Encourage the child to feel the material, pick it up, let it go, squeeze it and so on. Use the appropriate vocabulary. Once she has explored a few different textures, let her choose what she wants. For example:

◆ carpet pieces;*
◆ underlay;
◆ velvet;
◆ fur;
◆ suede;
◆ leather;
◆ nylon;
◆ cotton;
◆ wool;
◆ foam;
◆ sponges;
◆ foam balls;
◆ cotton wool;

- felt;
- rubber;
- plastic;
- kitchen scourers;*
- rubber balls;
- squeezy toys;
- Koosh ball: this is a special kind of ball that is easy to catch and pleasant to feel; it is available from many toy shops;
- Krinks ball: similar to the Koosh, but crinkly;
- a mixture of textures.

Take special care or avoid using the objects marked * when working with any child who has a tight or sudden grip, as they may hurt her. For example, a child with cerebral palsy may not be able to hold something lightly, or let go of an object she does not like.

Please make sure everything is clean.

Remember that the child does not have to feel anything — if she finds something unpleasant, take it away.

TACTILE EXPLORATION ACTIVITIES
Toiletries

You will need:

an aerosol can of 'ozone-friendly' shaving foam; child's apron or overall (optional); a shallow-sided tray (optional, but a tray saves the table or other surface from getting marked).

Useful words and phrases:

touch; feel; foam; smooth; foamy; white.

What to do

1. Sit the child at a table, so she can comfortably reach it, or the tray if you use one.

2. Shake the can well, and squeeze the shaving foam onto the table or into the tray.

3. Encourage the child to put her hands into the foam.

4. Sit back and allow her to explore, but do not let her eat the foam.

5. After a while you can join in, showing her different activities and talking about what you are both doing. If necessary, guide her hands, so that she explores as much as possible.

Variations

◆ Increase or decrease the amount of foam.

◆ Squeeze foam onto the child's hands.

◆ Show her how to do different things, such as make finger-trails or draw in the foam, rub or clap her hands together, dab it on her nose or ears, and so on.

Similar activities

You can do similar activities with a range of toiletries. Again, a tray and apron would be useful for most of these. Encourage the child to explore in her own way, taking care to keep most products away from her eyes, mouth and nose. Use the appropriate vocabulary. Once she has explored a few different toiletries, let her choose what she wants. For example:

◆ hand and body creams;

◆ talcum powder;

◆ baby oil;

◆ hair gel;

◆ hair mousse;

◆ facial masks (especially ones with interesting textures, such as oatmeal);

◆ Vaseline;

◆ Brylcreme.

TACTILE EXPLORATION ACTIVITIES
Soft & Sticky Foods

What to do

1 Make sure the child's hands are clean.

2 Sit her where she can comfortably reach the tray on a table.

3 Put the spaghetti into the tray.

4 Encourage her to put her hands in the spaghetti.

5 Sit back and allow her to explore.

6 After a while you can join in, showing her different activities and talking about what you are both doing. If necessary, guide her hands, so that she can explore as much as possible.

7 Wash and dry her hands afterwards.

! **Keep 'working trays' separate from mealtime equipment if you do not want the child to eat the food. This way she will learn that it is a different activity.**

You will need:

cold, cooked spaghetti; a fairly deep-sided tray; child's apron or overall; plastic knife or spoon (optional); pastry cutter or food mould (optional).

Useful words and phrases:

spaghetti; tray; cold; sticky; long; thin; pull; cut.

Variations

◆ Increase or decrease the amount of spaghetti.

◆ Vary the temperature, within reason.

◆ Show the child how to do different things: to pull the spaghetti apart, twirl it, make mounds and hollows in it, pull it to pieces, make patterns, and so on.

◆ Use the plastic knife or spoon to cut up the spaghetti and make patterns (do not use the spoon if the child is likely to think this means she can eat it).

◆ Use the pastry cutter or mould to make shapes.

71

Similar activities

You can carry out similar activities with a wide variety of foods. Encourage the child to explore in her own way, but if you are going to allow tasting/eating, do this before you have handled the food too much. Once the child has tried a few different textures, let her choose what she wants. For example:

◆ mousse;
◆ jelly;
◆ artificial cream (in an aerosol can);
◆ cream;
◆ dough;
◆ cake mixture;
◆ ice-cream;
◆ softened chocolate;
◆ mashed or blended potato;
◆ cooked rice;
◆ cooked pasta;
◆ mushy peas;
◆ soft fruits (orange, banana, kiwi and so on) sliced or mashed;
◆ raisins, sultanas, and so on, especially if they are stuck together.

(!) Please be clear and consistent about whether or not the child is allowed to eat or taste the foods. If eating is allowed, use ordinary plates and bowls for this activity. If not, use separate 'working-trays'.

If you do not want the child to eat the food, but she is at the stage of mouthing everything and cannot understand that she should not eat it, it is best not to mix up touching and tasting activities in the same session. You may even choose to leave these activities until she is a little older.

TACTILE EXPLORATION ACTIVITIES
Modelling Materials

What to do

1 Sit the child where she can comfortably reach the table or tray.

2 Give her some putty or put it in front of her.

3 Sit back and let her explore.

4 After a while you can join in and show her different things to do with the putty. Talk about what you are both doing. If necessary, guide her hands, so that she can explore as much as possible.

Variations

◆ Vary the size and amount of putty.

◆ Show the child different actions: pull it, stretch it, make thumb prints and finger prints, press it, roll it out with the hands, squeeze it back into a ball, and so on.

◆ Introduce shape-cutters, templates, plastic knife, rolling pin, and so on.

Similar activities

You can carry out similar activities with a range of substances found in many toy, art and hardware shops. Some of these brand-names are exclusive to particular shops or companies, and may change over time. Once the child has tried out a few different substances, let her choose what she wants. For example:

◆ Soft Stuff,
◆ Playdoh,
◆ Silicone or Silly Putty,
◆ plasticine,
◆ clay,
◆ paste,
◆ glue,
◆ Blu-Tack or Hold-it,
◆ dough.

You will need:

a large ball of putty, softened a little in your hands; tray (optional); shape-cutters (optional).

Useful words and phrases:

putty; squeeze; stretch; roll; break; pull; hands; thumb; finger(s); print; cut.

73

TACTILE EXPLORATION ACTIVITIES
Dry Textures

You will need:

a bag of clean sawdust; deep-sided tray; spoon; beaker and jug (optional).

Useful words and phrases:

sawdust; tray; feel; hold; sprinkle; pour.

What to do

1 Sit the child where she can comfortably reach the tray on the table.

2 Pour some sawdust into the tray.

3 Encourage her to put her hands in the sawdust.

4 Sit back and allow her to explore.

5 After a while you can join in, show her different things to do and talk about what you are both doing. If necessary, guide her hands, so that she explores as much as possible.

Variations

◆ Vary the amount of sawdust.

◆ Show the child different activities, such as making patterns in the sawdust, picking up handfuls of sawdust and sprinkling it back into the tray.

◆ Use the beaker to scoop up the sawdust.

◆ Use the spoon to scoop sawdust into the beaker, and so on.

◆ Use the jug to pour from one thing to another.

 Do not use sawdust with a child who has asthma or an allergy. With other children, test their reaction with a small amount first.

Similar activities

You can carry out similar activities with lots of different things, most of which can be found at home or bought cheaply. Once the child has explored a few textures, let her choose what she wants. For example:

◆ dry flour;
◆ dry rice;
◆ dry pasta and spaghetti;
◆ dry lentils, peas and beans*;
◆ dry cereals;
◆ straw;
◆ dry leaves;

- wood shavings;
- pot-pourri;
- dry sand;
- fresh, dry soil;
- polystyrene chips;
- clean packaging material;
- clean household junk (for example, kitchen-roll tubes; empty packets; wrapping paper; plastic bottles).

 Supervise the child closely, to make sure she puts nothing in her mouth, nose, ears, and so on.

Beware of using substances harmful to children who have asthma, hay fever or other allergies.

Make sure all materials are clean.

Soil should be dry, fresh, clean and free of stones, mini-beasts, and so on, not from the garden. If in doubt, do not use it.

Never use red kidney beans, as they are poisonous before soaking and cooking.

What to do

1 Sit the child where she can comfortably reach the table or tray.

2 Put the crackly paper in front of her.

3 Encourage her to feel the paper and to listen to it.

4 Sit back and allow her to explore.

5 After a while, join in and show her different ways to explore. Talk about what you are both doing. If necessary, guide her hands, so that she explores as much as possible.

Variations

◆ Vary the amount of crackly paper.

◆ Help the child to squeeze it close to her ears.

◆ Show her different actions: scrunching the paper up in the hands; banging it; twisting it with both hands, and so on.

Similar activities

You can carry out similar activities with a huge range of toys and equipment. The important point is that they make a noise when touched or handled in a very simple way, and that they stop making the noise when they are not being touched. For example:

◆ silver foil;

◆ scrunchy plastic (for example, plastic bags cut up into small pieces, chocolate box trays);

◆ squeaky toys and balls;

◆ rolling balls with a bell inside;

◆ bells and buzzers;

◆ activity centres;

◆ very simple musical instruments, such as a drum, washboard, shaker;

◆ 'bubble' packaging that 'pops';

◆ very dry leaves;

◆ tissue paper.

You will need:

some crackly paper, such as is used for the insides of boxes of chocolates; a deep-sided tray (optional).

Useful words and phrases:

paper; noisy; crackly; squeeze; both hands; listen.

TACTILE EXPLORATION ACTIVITIES

Visually Interesting Objects

What to do

1 Sit the child where she can comfortably reach the tray or table, if these are to be used. You can also do this activity with the child sitting on the floor.

2 Put one of the garlands on her lap, into the tray, or on the table, as preferred.

3 Encourage her to feel the garland and look at it.

4 Sit back and let her explore.

5 After a while, join in and show her different things to do. Talk about what you are both doing. If necessary, guide her hands, so that she can explore as much as possible.

You will need:

several shiny Christmas garlands; a deep-sided tray (optional).

Useful words and phrases:

Christmas; garland; shiny; silver; gold; soft; long; look; pretty; names of colours.

Variations

◆ Try a range of garlands of different colours and textures, one at a time.

◆ Give the child all the garlands at once.

◆ Run the garland through her hand(s) or show her how to do it.

◆ Twirl it in the light.

◆ Put it around her neck (with care).

Similar activities

You can carry out similar activities with other materials and objects that are colourful, shiny or look interesting in some way. Do not forget to vary the textures, too. When the child has tried a few toys, let her choose what she wants. For example:

◆ tinsel;

◆ Christmas decorations;

◆ Christmas tree decorations (be careful of any baubles that might break easily);

◆ silver foil;

◆ shiny paper;

◆ the silver insides of wine boxes (cleaned);

- hologram paper (this can be bought from art shops, or sometimes as wrapping paper);
- refraction paper (also from art or gift shops);
- coloured see-through thin plastic;
- sequinned material (but make sure the sequins do not come off or get swallowed);
- glowing objects and toys;
- mirrors;
- activity centres;
- cling film pictures (put blobs of paint or coloured oils between two pieces of cling film and watch them spread as you touch them);
- silver foil survival blankets (also called space blankets — buy in camping shops): these are quite large and can be wrapped around the child, or you can flap them up and down, and so on.

TACTILE EXPLORATION ACTIVITIES
Cause & Effect

What to do

1 Sit the child where she can easily reach the mobile.

2 Encourage her to touch, pat or hold the mobile, to make it move or stop moving. Make sure there are no draughts — it must be the child who causes the mobile to move.

3 Talk about what you are both doing.

Variations

◆ Tie a textured string or pull to the toy, so the child has to pull the string to make the mobile move.

◆ Use different kinds of mobiles, but not delicate ones that might break if handled: they can be made from all sorts of materials, such as wood, plastic, foam, plush, fur, and so on.

Similar activities

You can carry out similar activities with a wide range of toys. The important point is that the toys or objects should do something as a result of being touched or handled in a very simple way. Once the child has tried a few toys, let her choose what she wants. For example:

◆ push-button toys (for example, telephone, cash register, cars);

◆ lever toys (such as pop-up toys);

◆ activity centres;

◆ simple musical instruments;

◆ gimmicky toys: for example, there is a ball that laughs when banged, and one that makes the sound of glass smashing when thrown (look around the gift and joke shops where you can buy 'adult' executive toys);

◆ hand, foot and finger painting;

◆ toys operated using a simple single switch (needing only a light touch on the switch);

◆ computer games operated by a single switch (needing only a light touch);

◆ computer games operated with a touch-screen (the child only has to touch the special screen placed over the monitor);

◆ textured switches: put interesting textures onto the switches to encourage touching.

You will need:

a mobile: this could look, feel, sound or even smell nice.

Useful words and phrases:

mobile; hang(ing); touch; hit; swing(ing); stop; look; listen; up; high; over; above.

TACTILE EXPLORATION ACTIVITIES
Shapes

You will need:

several medium-sized, hard, smooth, square bricks all the same colour; a deep-sided tray (optional, but if you use one you will not have to pick up the bricks so often).

Useful words and phrases:

brick; square; shape; feel; corner; hard; soft; rough; smooth; big; small; names of colours.

What to do

1 Sit the child where she can comfortably reach the table or tray.

2 Put one brick into the tray.

3 Encourage the child to feel the brick, first with one hand and then with both hands.

4 Sit back and let her explore.

5 After a while you can join in and make sure she is really feeling the shape of the brick — its corners and surfaces, and so on. Talk about what you are both doing. If necessary, guide her hands, so that she explores as much as possible.

Variations

Keep to the same shape — a square — but vary the other aspects:

◆ use a larger or smaller brick;

◆ vary the texture: wood, fur, plastic, and so on;

◆ vary the colour, or mix colours up;

◆ vary the flexibility: foam, rubber, wood, and so on.

Similar activities

You can carry out similar activities with other objects. You must concentrate on one shape at a time to begin with, but can explore everything that occurs in that shape. Consider the shape from both a three-dimensional (solid) and a two-dimensional (flat) viewpoint. For example, the child could feel a solid ball, and the flat shape of a ball, made out of foam. Go on to feeling and seeing the differences between shapes.

Examples of shapes:

◆ square,
◆ circle,
◆ triangle,
◆ rectangle (oblong),
◆ diamond,
◆ oval,

◆ semi-circle,
◆ star,
◆ moon (crescent).

Examples of shapes in everyday objects:

◆ *square:* bricks; books; boxes; table-top; toy house; greeting card; toy shapes;
◆ *circle:* balls; baubles; chocolate buttons; globe; the rim of a cup; number zero; the letter 'O' (these can be made from textured materials);
◆ *triangle:* musical triangle; pyramid; toy shapes; a certain chocolate box;
◆ *rectangle:* as for square.

TACTILE EXPLORATION ACTIVITIES
People

You will need:

just yourself.

**Useful words
and phrases:**

*touch; don't touch;
feel; skin; hair; names
of body parts; private;
public; no.*

What to do

1 The child can sit anywhere for this activity.

2 Hold hands with the child.

3 Encourage her to explore every part of your hand(s) with both of her own.

4 Talk about what you are both doing. If necessary, guide her hands, so that she can explore as much as possible.

5 Remember that the object is for the child to explore *your* hands and face, not the other way round.

Variations

◆ Encourage the child to explore your face, hair, neck, feet, clothes, and so on.

◆ Encourage her to explore her own face, hair, and so on.

◆ Use hand-cream, face-paints, make-up, face masks, hair-spray, and so on, to make this more purposeful and more fun.

! **Unless you are the child's parents, or equivalent, do not touch the private parts of the child's body, or let her touch the private parts of yours. *It is important to distinguish between appropriate and inappropriate touching.***
Make sure your behaviour cannot be misinterpreted. For your own protection, do not carry out this activity when you are alone with the child.

82

Early Sensory Skills

TACTILE EXPLORATION ACTIVITIES

Whole Body Experiences

What to do

1 Make sure the water is comfortably warm, and take the child out of the pool immediately she shows any sign of getting cold.

2 Gradually introduce the child into the water. Be gentle and non-threatening. Encourage her to sit down, put her hands in, lie down on her back or front, and so on. If possible, get in with the child to make her feel safer.

3 Talk about what you are both doing.

4 Encourage her to move in the water and splash. Trickle water gently over different parts of her body, naming them.

5 As she gets used to it, you can become more boisterous.

6 Dry off thoroughly when you have finished.

7 Remove the water immediately to avoid accidents.

Variations

◆ Put bubble bath, foam or colour into the water.
◆ Put water toys and containers into the pool.
◆ Use bubbles while playing in the water.

 Never leave young children unsupervised in or near water.

Unless you are the child's parents or usual carers, it may be wise not to carry out this activity when working alone with the child.

Similar activities

You can carry out similar activities with a wide range of equipment. Unfortunately, most ordinary homes and clinics do not have much large apparatus. However, many nurseries, playgroups, schools and leisure centres do, and it is worthwhile using their facilities now and again, as they give the child new

You will need:

a paddling-pool; garden or outdoor area to put it in; towel; swimming-costume (optional); water toys and bubbles (optional); armbands (optional); a warm day.

Useful words and phrases:

get undressed; water; pool; stand; paddle; sit (down); splash; lie (down); in; over; wet; finished; out; dry; towel; get dressed; names of body parts.

and interesting experiences. Some equipment encourages relaxation, while some encourages active physical play; both are necessary. For example:

◆ ball pool: a pool full of light, plastic balls that a child can sink into;

◆ soft play and similar environments: these are padded areas with soft, foam-filled equipment, such as tunnels, steps and swings;
◆ inflatables such as 'wobbly castles';
◆ water-bed and vibrating bed: these are often found in specialized soft play environments.

You can also provide similar experiences easily and cheaply at home with a few materials (see also Section 4, 'Everyday Activities'). For example:

◆ sand pits;
◆ textured tunnels;
◆ tactile mats and floor surfaces (make your own, using interesting and varied textures);
◆ tactile boxes to sit in (make your own, using interesting and varied textures);
◆ box or pool full of polystyrene chips;
◆ space blankets, sheets, netting, net curtains, shawls and blankets to cover the body or go over the head like a tent.

Once the child has tried a few activities, let her choose what she wants to do.

 All of these activities require close supervision.

Tactile Exploration
CHECKLIST

Child's name	

Date	Activity		Comments/Responses
	Tactile Exploration	Materials and Textures	
		Toiletries	
		Soft and Sticky Foods	
		Modelling Materials	
		Dry Textures	
		Noisy Objects	
		Visually Interesting Objects	
		Cause and Effect	
		Shapes	
		People	
		Whole Body Experiences	
		Child's Preferred Activities	

TASTE AND SMELL

SECTION 3

INTRODUCTION

THE IMPORTANCE of taste and smell to cognitive development and language acquisition has often been overlooked. However, smelling, mouthing and tasting are amongst the earliest ways that infants explore their environment. For many children with sensory and learning disabilities, they remain of primary importance.

Tasting and smelling activities are necessary for teaching specific vocabulary, such as the concept of 'sweetness'. It would be very difficult for anyone to understand this if they had never tasted a sweet food or contrasted it with other flavours.

Tasting can be included in oral exercises as part of an oral and articulation programme to encourage lip and tongue movements. It can also be used to stimulate the sense of taste, to promote an interest in eating and to practise good feeding skills. Seek advice from appropriate sources, such as speech and language clinicians, physiotherapists and dieticians, before starting such programmes.

Tasting and smelling are very enjoyable and can raise the interest of even the most profoundly delayed child. They therefore make useful motivators and rewards to help some children attempt other activities.

Aims

1 To stimulate the child.

2 To encourage her interest in the person providing the experiences.

3 To encourage interaction between the child and her carer.

4 To encourage communication between the child and her carer.

5 To build up concepts about objects.

6 To give opportunities for the child to express preferences, likes and dislikes.

7 To give opportunities for the child to make and communicate choices about what she wants.

8 To help learn appropriate vocabulary.

9 To motivate the child to achieve other activities (optional).

AWARENESS OF TASTE

Additional aims

1 To raise the child's awareness of, and interest in, her sense of taste.

2 To raise her interest in food and drink.

3 To motivate the child to do oral exercises, as part of an articulation programme (optional).

4 To motivate the child to eat, as part of an eating and drinking programme (optional).

Hints

1 Take appropriate food safety and hygiene precautions.

2 Keep all foods in the right storage conditions; throw away any past their use-by date and any that look or smell suspicious.

3 Have plenty of clean crockery and cutlery available.

4 Make sure you and the child wash your hands before and after activities — and during them if necessary.

5 Have a drink of water available, to stop the child's mouth getting dry and to clear her palate between different tastes.

6 Make sure her mouth is clean after tasting activities: give her a drink or clean her teeth.

7 Try and keep a balance of different food types, bearing in mind nutrition, additives and quantities.

8 Be aware of the child's diet, including any special or cultural diets, and any allergies she may suffer from.

Remember!

◆ Always encourage the child's attempts to communicate.

◆ Try using the useful words.

◆ Respect the child's likes and dislikes, but do not make assumptions about them — let her try things out. Some children do enjoy spicy tastes or lemon juice!

◆ Be careful how you interpret the child's responses. They may not mean what you think they mean; for example, a child who grimaces on eating ice-cream may really love it, but react to the cold. Look for a combination of responses: for example, does she open or close her mouth for the next spoonful?

◆ Respond to the child's choices and preferences.

◆ Be aware of the child's health, mood and appetite generally, and during the session itself.

◆ Make sure you know about any eating or drinking problems.

◆ Please consult physiotherapists and speech and language clinicians whenever you do activities involving food and drink with children with poor posture and/or eating difficulties.

AWARENESS OF TASTE ACTIVITIES
Contrasting Tastes

What to do

1 Make sure you and the child are comfortable. She should always be in a good position for eating, even if you are only going to give tiny amounts of food or drink.

2 Offer a small taste of sweet food and note the child's responses. Offer a little more.

3 Offer a small drink of water to clear the taste, and a tissue to wipe the mouth.

4 Do the same with the savoury food.

5 Offer a choice between the two tastes.

6 Look out for any responses that may indicate lack of appetite, like, dislike, 'not now, thank you', or 'more, please'. These include: turning towards or away from the spoon; opening or closing her mouth; shaking her head; smiling; laughing; grimacing (not necessarily a sign of dislike); taking your hand or the spoon and pulling it nearer, or pushing it away; vocalizing and so on.

7 Chat to the child throughout the activity.

You will need:

one sweet taste; one savoury taste; two spoons or tongue-depressors for tasting; jug of water; tissues.

Useful words and phrases:

drink; food; taste; sweet; savoury; more; enough; like; don't like.

Variations

◆ Contrast two different types of taste, such as sweet and savoury; sour and salty; sharp and bland; bitter and spicy; and so on.

◆ Contrast two different textures, such as wet and dry; hard and soft; spongy or melt-in-the-mouth and crunchy; and so on.

◆ Contrast two different temperatures from: hot; warm; tepid; cool; cold or frozen.

◆ Contrast raw versus cooked foods, such as carrot; apple; cabbage; tomato; cake mixture.

◆ Contrast two drinks, for example, hot and cold; flat and fizzy; thick and watery; strong and weak.

◆ Contrast different food types, such as meat and vegetables; bread and fruit; and so on.

Similar activities

Below are ideas for contrasting tastes, textures and drinks.

Different tastes:

Sweet	Savoury	Sour/Sharp	Spicy
chocolate	brown sauce	pickle	paprika
honey	cheese	lemon	curry
syrup	peanut butter	kiwi fruit	chilli sauce
jam		plain yogurt	garlic
sugar		mint sauce	
peach chutney		mango chutney	
apple sauce		pineapple	

Salty	Bland	Bitter
crisps	plain potato	thick-cut marmalade
smoked bacon	plain white bread	beer
kippers	plain boiled rice	bitter lemon
	plain pancake	grapefruit
	plain boiled fish	pomegranate

Wet/Sticky	Dry	Hard	Soft/Spongy
custard	biscuit	raw carrot	sponge cake
jelly	wafer	hard mints	sponge fingers
trifle	cornflakes	boiled sweets	mashed potato
yogurt	nuts	toffee	banana
ice-cream		apple	mashed yam
			pureed parsnips

Different textures:

Melt-in-the mouth	Smooth	Crunchy
crispy prawn crackers	smooth peanut butter	crunchy peanut butter
chocolate	plain yogurt	crisp lettuce
	mousse	cereals
	cream cheese	coleslaw
		crisp fruit
		poppadoms

Different drinks:

Hot	Cold	Flat	Fizzy	Thick
tea	iced tea	fresh juice	Coca-Cola	milk shake
coffee	water	lemon squash	Lucozade	milky coffee
milk	milk	tap water	Perrier	thick soup
hot chocolate	orange juice	lemon barley water		thick fresh juice
hot juices	mango juice			

Please be careful! Certain foods are not suitable for young children and those with eating difficulties: for example, peanuts, which are easily swallowed and may cause choking.

Food allergies are an increasing problem. If you are not the child's usual carer, make sure you find out what she can and cannot eat. Avoid foods with known risks, such as peanuts.

AWARENESS OF SMELL

Additional aims

1 To raise the child's awareness of, and interest in, her sense of smell.

2 To raise her interest in food and drink.

AWARENESS OF SMELL ACTIVITIES
Aromatic Experiences

What to do

1 Make sure you and the child are comfortable.

2 Hold an open perfume bottle under her nose for a few seconds, without spraying.

3 Spray the air a foot or two away from the child — always spray away from the face.

4 Put dabs of perfume on her wrist or the back of her hand, and help her smell it.

5 Put some behind her ears or on her neck, and so on.

6 Make sure she gets several sniffs.

7 Talk to the child all the time, and note her responses, such as wrinkling her nose, or pulling the bottle nearer to smell it, and so on.

8 Try the other smells. You may need to blow away the first scent with a fan to clear the air.

You will need:

scent; perfume; after-shave; and so on.

Useful words and phrases:

smell; scent; perfume; after-shave; nose; spray; flowery; fruity; like; don't like; strong.

Variations

◆ Contrast two different smells: for example, spray one hand with strawberry perfume, and one with after-shave; do not soak the air or she will not be able to tell the difference.

◆ Offer the child a choice between two different smells.

Similar activities

Similar activities can be carried out with all sorts of smells. For example:

◆ scented hand and body lotions and creams;
◆ scented oils;
◆ scented candles;
◆ incense and joss-sticks;

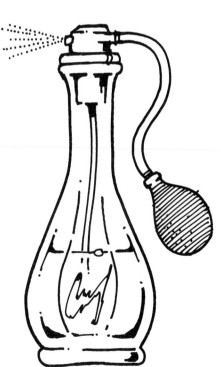

Section 3: Taste and Smell

- scented light-bulbs (put the scent on the bulb);
- fresh-air sprays;
- room fresheners, including plug-in varieties;
- use fans to waft scent around the room;
- flavourings and essences that are used in cooking, such as peppermint, rum, butterscotch, and so on;
- jars of food, especially spreads (smell from spoons, not the jars themselves);
- essential oils, used for aromatherapy.

Taste and Smell
CHECKLIST

Child's name	

Date	Activity	Comments/Responses
	Awareness of Taste	
	Awareness of Smell	
	Preferred Tastes	
	Preferred Textures	
	Preferred Drinks	
	Preferred Smells	

EVERYDAY ACTIVITIES

SECTION 4

INTRODUCTION

I N THIS section are some lists of everyday activities that focus on vision, touch, taste and smell. Many ordinary activities that we take for granted are, in fact, rich sensory experiences, often involving the whole body. When we carry them out with children we should try to emphasize the sensory aspects of the experience and make them aware of the appropriate vocabulary.

The activities may also be used to motivate children, and as rewards for other achievements. They provide good opportunities for encouraging children to make and communicate choices.

These everyday activities are especially important for children with physical disabilities, who spend a good deal of their time in hard seating, side supports and standing-frames. This reduces their opportunities for close contact with people and their experience of different surfaces. Such children should be involved in sensory activities every day, both to enjoy personal contact and affection, and to interact with the environment.

Aims

1 To stimulate the child.

2 To relax the child.

3 To raise the child's awareness of, and interest in, the senses of sight, touch, taste and smell.

4 To help the child to learn about her body and develop body image.

5 To develop relationships between the child and her carer.

6 To encourage interaction and communication between the child and her carer.

7 To help the child learn about the environment.

8 To help the child build up concepts about objects.

9 To give opportunities for the child to express preferences and make choices.

Remember!

◆ Always encourage the child's attempts to communicate.

◆ Emphasize the sensory experience.

◆ Try to teach the appropriate vocabulary.

◆ Respect the child and her privacy.

◆ Respect her likes and dislikes, choices and preferences, and respond to them.

◆ Do not make assumptions about her likes and dislikes — let her try things out.

◆ Be aware of safety and hygiene considerations, and know how to deal with any potentially dangerous situations, such as in the swimming pool.

◆ Remember that all the warnings given in the previous sections still apply to everyday activities.

◆ Do some of these activities every day.

EVERYDAY ACTIVITIES
Vision

This section lists everyday activities that involve and emphasize the sense of sight. For example:

Outside the home:

- going to a funfair, circus, carnival or parade;
- watching clowns, acrobats, tumblers, jugglers and so on;
- watching, or going on, swings, slide, roundabout, and so on;
- fireworks displays;
- flying kites, especially where there are lots in one place, as at kite festivals;
- letting balloons go up into the air, especially where there are a lot, as in a balloon race at a fete;
- going to see a show, dance, ice-dance or other kind of spectacular;
- going to the zoo, farm or pet corner;
- some museums have good visual effects: for example, science museums often have moving exhibits; cultural museums have interesting visual displays, such as ethnic and historic homes, clothes, jewellery, artefacts, masks, tapestries, and so on;
- animated waxwork displays, especially those with famous figures;
- some painting, sculpture and textile exhibitions are interesting and suitable for children, especially if they encourage touching as well as looking;
- Christmas time gives rise to lots of colourful displays and occasions, such as shows, pantomimes, Christmas lights, parties, decorated shops and trees, and so on;
- going to the cinema;
- going to the seaside, especially when there are big waves;
- going to the countryside, especially when there are great areas of colour to see, such as bluebell woods, or fields of poppies;
- watching the wind ripple through trees, grass or cornfields, and so on;
- walking in the park or in flower gardens;
- watching clouds and aeroplanes move across the sky;
- watching boats moving through water;
- walking down the street, looking at traffic, and so on;
- going into shops;
- generally going out and having a change of environment.

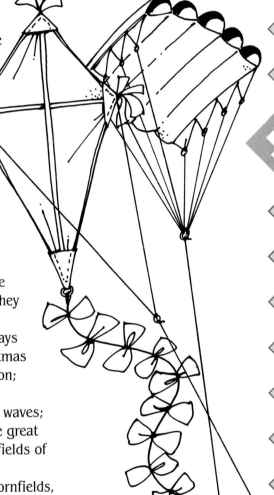

105

Around the home:

◆ watching television programmes or videos, especially if they are colourful or have fascinating special effects;

◆ looking out of the window;

◆ looking at people, pets, flowers and birds;

◆ watching lights, lamps and torches going on and off;

◆ watching doors, windows, curtains and cupboards opening and closing;

◆ watching mobiles, wind-chimes, automatic fans and clocks (especially cuckoo clocks or those with pendulums);

◆ watching water: for example, going into the bath, down the plug-hole, flushing the toilet, or coming out of the shower;

◆ looking at shadows;

◆ watching house and garden appliances, such as the vacuum cleaner, dishwasher, washing-machine, tumble-drier, iron, knitting machine, saw, sander, lawnmower, and so on;

◆ watching curtains, vertical blinds, bead or plastic-strip curtains blowing in the breeze;

◆ looking at old cinefilms or slide shows;

◆ watching fibre-optic lamps, oil-lamps, music-boxes, executive toys and so on;

◆ watching people's everyday actions and movements: for example, doing the housework or the gardening, cooking, walking, jumping, dancing, doing exercises, playing games and sports, walking on stilts, pogo-ing, clapping hands, and so on.

Remember not to overstimulate children who have epilepsy or visual sensitivity, as flashing lights and similar effects can bring on epileptic attacks and/or headaches.

EVERYDAY ACTIVITIES
Touch

This section lists everyday activities that involve and emphasize the sense of touch. For example:

Outside the home:
◆ going to the beach, playing in the sand and sea;
◆ paddling pools and swimming baths;
◆ going in a jacuzzi;
◆ going to a sauna or Turkish bath;
◆ going to a solarium, or using sunbeds;
◆ being in the sun, sunbathing;
◆ being in the rain, splashing in puddles;
◆ feeling the breeze and wind;
◆ playing in the snow, snowfights, making snowmen;
◆ playing in mud, making mud-pies;
◆ walking barefoot;
◆ going for walks in the country; nature trails; feeling the trees, plants, grass, and so on;
◆ agility activities such as crawling through tunnels; wriggling under blankets and netting; rolling or bouncing on large balls; being swung in blankets; playing balloon and ball-games, and so on;

◆ using inflatables and bouncy castles;
◆ using soft play areas and special multisensory environments;
◆ using slides and waterchutes;
◆ rolling on the floor, down hills, and so on;
◆ going to the hairdressers;
◆ having a massage.

Around the home:
◆ playing under garden hoses and sprinklers;
◆ having a shower or bath;
◆ using a sunlamp or sunbed;
◆ being in the sun, sunbathing;
◆ lying and sitting on different textures, such as rugs, sheepskins, beanbags, hard or soft chairs, and so on;
◆ wearing clothes of varied textures;
◆ wearing furry hats, muffs and stoles;
◆ using make-up, nail-varnish, toiletries, and so on;

107

- having your hair done;
- having a massage;
- cuddling, hugging, holding hands, kissing;
- tickling and tickle games;
- stroking pets;
- playing with cuddly toys, activity mats, activity centres, activity boards;
- playing with glove puppets;
- hand, foot and finger painting; face paints;
- modelling with clay, and so on;
- making collages and junk models;
- preparing and cooking food.

(!) Remember to take care how you carry out massage and other bodily activities, or allow other people to do so. Always ask for the school's or nursery's guidelines, if they have them.

This section lists everyday activities that emphasize the sense of taste, and also involve the sense of smell. For example:

◆ cooking (and eating);
◆ eating out;
◆ picnics;
◆ parties;
◆ feasts and festivals.

There are some foods that can be simply made, without a cooker. For example:

◆ jelly;
◆ cheesecake-mix;
◆ milkshakes;
◆ cold drinks;
◆ cola-floats;
◆ open and closed sandwiches;
◆ snacks and titbits;
◆ cereals;
◆ raw vegetables and dips;
◆ fruit salad;
◆ fruit fools;
◆ salads.

There are 'exciting' foods that substantially change their appearance when made. For example:

◆ jelly, soufflé, ice-cream, mousse, fruit fool;
◆ popcorn;
◆ cakes, shaped sweets and biscuits;
◆ grated and melted cheese;
◆ pressurized 'cream' in aerosols;
◆ poppadoms, prawn crackers;
◆ pasta, rice, noodles;
◆ dumplings;
◆ eggs;
◆ batter mixture (into pancakes);
◆ spun fruits (such as toffee-apples) and candy-floss;
◆ tortillas;
◆ dips (from liquidized foods);
◆ mussels, prawns (look very different out of their shells);
◆ custard and gravy from powders;
◆ potatoes into chips and mash, and so on;
◆ melon into melon balls;

- fresh fruit into fruit crushes;
- frozen juices;
- put toppings on plain pizzas;
- meat into mince and then to burgers.

Remember to take precautions to avoid food allergies, sickness and choking. If you do not have first aid skills yourself, make sure you know who to call in an emergency.

EVERYDAY ACTIVITIES
Smell

This section lists everyday activities that involve and emphasize the sense of smell. For example:

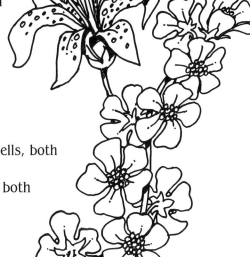

◆ smelling flowers and garden plants;
◆ visiting well-known gardens and horticultural centres;
◆ visiting herb-gardens and special scented gardens;
◆ having fresh flowers, fruit or pot-pourri around the house;
◆ using room fresheners or fresh-air sprays;
◆ lighting candles, especially scented ones;
◆ going on a nature walk, smelling country smells, both pleasant and unpleasant;
◆ going on a town walk, smelling town smells, both pleasant and unpleasant;
◆ using toiletries, having a bath, and so on;
◆ using massage oils and aromatherapy oils;
◆ cooking;
◆ going out to restaurants, or even just passing them in the street.

Everyday Activities
CHECKLIST

Child's name	

Date	Activity	Comments/Responses
	Vision	
	Preferred Visual Activities	
	Touch	
	Preferred Tactile Activities	
	Taste	
	Preferred Taste Activities	
	Smell	
	Preferred Smell Activities	
	Likes	
	Dislikes	

GAMES

SECTION 5

INTRODUCTION

THE FOLLOWING games are meant to encourage awareness of the senses in the older or more able child. Most of them are suitable for both one-to-one work and groups, while some are specifically for groups. They include games that many of us used to play when we were children and can be used as party games at home or in the classroom. They may be adapted for children with disabilities.

Aims

1 To have fun.

2 To encourage awareness of sight, touch, taste and smell.

3 To build up concepts about objects.

4 To encourage co-operative playing.

5 To encourage play between children.

6 To encourage communication.

7 To teach appropriate vocabulary.

8 To develop attention and concentration.

9 To integrate information from different senses.

Remember!

◆ These games are intended for the older or more able child.

◆ Many of them are suitable for both one-to-one work and groups.

- ◆ A few, mainly party games, are only for groups.
- ◆ They may be adapted for children with disabilities.
- ◆ You will need lots of space for some of these games, especially with groups of children.
- ◆ Make sure the room is clear of hazards.
- ◆ Always encourage the child's attempts to communicate.
- ◆ Try using the useful words.
- ◆ Have fun!

For tactile games, remember!

- ◆ The child needs to have practice in *seeing* the activities done, before she can rely entirely on the sense of touch.
- ◆ When she *is* trying to guess what they are solely by touch, she must not be able to see the objects, so provide a blindfold. (Never force a child to wear a blindfold. Some children, especially young ones, are very nervous of them.)
- ◆ Collect useful bags, boxes and so on for tactile and feeling activities. These can vary from see-through bags for getting the child used to activities, to quite thick opaque bags. Boxes should have a hole cut in the side to put the hands through.
- ◆ Encourage the child to describe what she can feel, if appropriate.
- ◆ Be aware of dangers, such as sharp objects, or rough textures that could cause allergies, and so on.

For taste and smell games, remember!

- ◆ Make sure you know about any eating or drinking problems.
- ◆ Take appropriate food safety and hygiene precautions.
- ◆ Be aware of any allergies, diet, special diets and cultural diets.

VISUAL GAMES
Early Toys

What to do

1. Choose a very simple toy to start with, that has only two or three basic shapes, such as circle, square and cross.

2. Show the child what to do with the toy.

3. Let her play with it in her own way for a little while — she may discover how to match the shapes by herself.

4. If not, show her how to take the shapes out — this is much easier than putting them in. Let her practise this new skill.

5. Give her one shape at a time to match to its hole. She will use a combination of vision and touch to find the right hole through trial and error. You can help as much as necessary, by doing one or all of the following: pointing to the right hole, turning the shape around for her, positioning the shape above the hole, partly placing it in the hole and letting her push it through, and so on.

6. The important point is that the child at least does the last bit so that she feels she has achieved and finished something.

Variations

◆ Give the child all the shapes at once.

◆ Point to a hole, and she must find the right shape.

◆ Pretend that you cannot find the right hole and let her help you.

◆ Gradually introduce harder toys, such as ones with lots of holes; more complex shapes; smaller pieces; or pieces of all one colour, so that there are no extra colour clues.

You will need:

a shape-sorter toy; that is, one where the child has to put shapes into matching holes.

Useful words and phrases:

shape; names of shapes; here; take them out; put it in; same; different; matching; finished; all done.

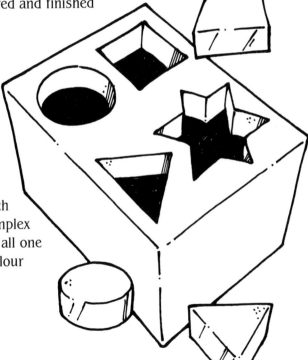

Similar activities

You can encourage attention to visual features and hand–eye co-ordination with lots of different toys and activities. Most are available in ordinary toy shops; educational catalogues are also a good source, especially once you want more complex toys. For example:

◆ shape inset trays: these are usually easier than the shape-sorters, and often have only two or three holes — you can even buy them with only one large shape;

◆ stacking toys, such as rings on a stick, cups that fit on top of each other, teddies and cats that pull apart and fit back together, and so on;

◆ nesting toys, such as Russian dolls, Father Christmases, barrels, cups and so on, that fit inside each other;

◆ size-grading toys: again toys that fit inside each other;

◆ large floor puzzles, that is ones with very large pieces;

◆ matching activities: you can buy games made specifically for this, but many of them involve pictures, which are usually harder than real objects; you can also use whatever toys and objects you already have, as long as there are at least two of them; useful toys are bricks, cars, balls, small dolls and teddies, books, pencils, and so on;

◆ sorting activities: you can buy sorting toys, but you could just as easily give the child a pile of toy bricks, or different coloured woollen pom-poms. It is natural for children at a certain stage to want to make order, and she will probably sort them into sizes and colours;

◆ activity centres: these have a number of different switches, buttons to push, strings to pull and so on, so the child has to learn which ones will operate her favourite parts of the toy;

◆ cause-and-effect and surprise toys, especially if there is more than one operation: for example, a button to make something appear and a lever to make it disappear again.

VISUAL GAMES
Table Top

What to do

1 Choose a simple set to start off with: that is, large dominoes with simple, bold, familiar pictures.

2 If this is a new game to the child, show her some of the matching pictures, name them, and just let her match them up for a little while.

3 Demonstrate the rules of the game and have a practice run.

4 Play the game.

Variations

◆ You can make the game shorter and easier by removing some of the dominoes, giving them all out at the beginning, or putting some sort of marker by the end pictures so that the child knows which ones she has to match.

◆ Gradually introduce harder games, with more complex and less familiar pictures.

◆ Dominoes can be played with a group of children.

Similar activities

You can encourage attention to visual features and hand–eye co-ordination with lots of different toys and games. Most are available in ordinary toy shops; educational catalogues are also a good source, especially once you want more complex toys. For example:

◆ Snap and other card games;

◆ Lotto games, Bingo and so on;

◆ odd-one-out: you need several sets of matching pictures; put two or three identical pictures and one odd one on the table and see if the child can spot the odd-one-out;

◆ playing with microscopes, telescopes, magnifying glasses and cameras;

◆ hand–eye co-ordination toys, such as duck-hooking and fishing games: there is a clockwork version, where the fish have magnetic pieces in their mouths which they open and close, while the child tries to catch them with a magnetic rod; this is available in shops in both small and large forms;

You will need:

a set of picture dominoes

Useful words and phrases:

dominoes; game; play; pictures; same; different; matching; your turn; my turn; have you got the same one?; can't go; finished.

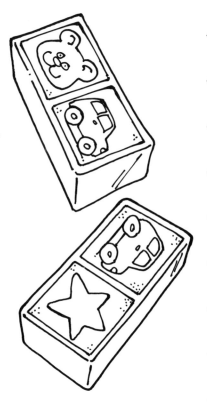

119

♦ construction toys, where the child builds something, or fits things together: examples are Duplo, Lego, pegmen, bricks, and various toys that involve making things from straws, cogs, discs and so on;

♦ jigsaw puzzles;

♦ games that involve observation and memory, such as the following:

'Kim's Game': some common objects or toys are put on a tray and shown to the child; then one or two are taken away and the child has to say which ones are gone;

variations of 'Kim's Game': for example, the child has to recall as many objects as possible from the tray; add one or two objects to a tray and see if the child spots them; change the positions of the objects and see if she can put them back in their original places, and so on;

'Pelmanism' or 'Pairs': you have two sets of identical pictures which you place face-down on the table; take it in turns to turn over two cards and see if they match; the winner is the one with the most matching pairs at the end. You can buy these games or make your own.

VISUAL GAMES
Active Play

What to do

1 Set up two or three skittles to start with.

2 Stand a few feet away and show the child how to knock them down.

3 Let her practise, getting as close as she needs to, even knocking them down with the ball still in her hand if necessary.

4 When she seems reasonably ready, take turns to have a game of skittles.

Variations

◆ Make it easier or harder by having more or fewer skittles; smaller or larger ball and skittles; standing nearer or further away; specifying rolling, throwing or bouncing actions; introducing a points system, and so on.

◆ Try it with your eyes closed.

◆ Try with one hand, two hands or kicking the ball.

◆ Play it as a group or team game, or make a competition out of it.

Similar activities

You can encourage attention to visual features and hand–eye co-ordination with lots of different games. For example:

◆ hoop-la, quoits and other games where you have to throw a ring over a stick or object, or onto a hook;

◆ target games where you have to aim for a specific object: for example, darts (use only sucker-tipped ones); tossing a beanbag into a hoop; 'beanbag-he', where the child 'catches' you by throwing a beanbag at your legs, and so on;

◆ all sorts of ball, and bat-and-ball games;

◆ hiding games such as 'Hunt the Thimble', where you hide something in the room or garden, and the child has to find it: you can give clues if you wish; use larger toys, pictures and objects to start off with, in easy places, and gradually get harder;

You will need:

a set of large skittles;
a large, soft ball.

Useful words and phrases:

skittles; ball; put them up;
knock them down/over;
my turn; your turn;
pick it up.

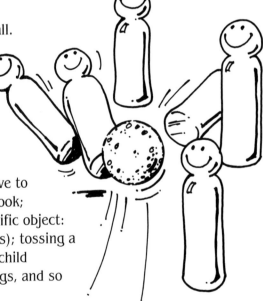

121

◆ imitation games such as the following:

'Follow my Leader': the child has to follow you around the room or garden, doing the same actions and walking the same way;

'Simple Simon Says' (also called 'O'Grady Says'): the child has to copy your actions, postures, sounds or facial expressions, but only if you first say, "Simple Simon says do this." If you only say, "Do this" and she copies you, she is 'out';

various songs, such as 'Incy-Wincy Spider', 'Wind the Bobbin up', 'Wheels on the Bus', 'Roly-poly, roly-poly', and so on, will encourage visual attention and memory (see Appendix II for the words and actions).

VISUAL GAMES
Party Games

What to do

1 Sit everyone in a circle and show them the butterfly.

2 Send a volunteer out of the room.

3 Pin the butterfly to one of the children's clothes. Give instructions to be as quiet as possible and not 'give the game away'.

4 Call the child back in and tell her she must 'spot the butterfly'. You can give clues if you wish: for example, tell her what colour hair the person with the butterfly has.

5 When the child has found the butterfly, someone else can go outside; continue until everyone has had a turn.

Variations

◆ Play the same game with all sorts of different objects, such as a badge, sticker, transfer or gummed shape; it does not have to be a butterfly — anything will do, the sillier the better, such as a rabbit, a flower, a foot, a false nose; current 'fads' are useful, such as characters from cartoons and so on.

◆ Make it easy to start with by using quite big objects, and putting them in obvious places, such as on top of the head, or pinned to the child's jumper.

◆ Make it harder by using very small objects and putting them in less obvious places, such as on the back of the child's knee or her elbow.

Similar activities

You can encourage observation and visual attention with lots of different games. For example:

◆ What's changed?: this is similar to the above game, in that one child leaves the room while one or more of the others changes something about their appearance, for example, taking off a shoe, swapping jumpers or putting on a hat. The child does not need good language skills to describe what has happened, as long as she can show she has noticed the difference;

You will need:

for 'Spot the Butterfly': a butterfly brooch, or picture or toy that you can fix onto yourself in some way, for example with Blu-Tack or Hold-it.

Useful words and phrases:

butterfly; game; play; outside; inside; spot the butterfly; where is it?; find/found; next.

- Charades: play a version of this popular game by giving simple things to mime: for instance, putting on socks, pouring a drink, waving good-bye, watching television, playing football, singing, and so on;
- role-play games: these can make a simple memory task much more interesting for the older child. For example, some children could pretend to be policemen and policewomen at the scene of a crime, while others are witnesses who try to describe what happened. Or you can pretend you are at the cinema. Show a little of a film or cartoon, have one child come in 'late', and the others must tell her what has happened so far. Another idea would be to copy television game shows where contestants are meant to remember 'prizes' they saw on a conveyor belt, or to recall details from a video. Keep it simple;
- 'Blindman's Buff'; 'Squeak, Piggy, Squeak'; 'Pin the Tail on the Donkey': these games bring home what it feels like *not* to see;
- 'Bunnies': this is a silly game that requires good attention. Everyone sits in a circle and says "Bunnies, bunnies, bunnies" and so on while they wiggle their hands in front of them. You start the game by wiggling your hands on top of your head like a rabbit's ears. The child on your left has to wiggle her *right* hand, while the child on your right wiggles her *left* hand, again like rabbits (but with only one ear!). After a few seconds, point to someone else, who has to make two bunny ears, while the children on either side wiggle their left or right hand. Meanwhile you and the first two children have returned to wiggling your hands in front of you. Carry on till everyone's been a 'bunny' or you are laughing too much to continue;
- 'Killer Wink': this is another daft game. Sit in a circle and give each child an envelope with a counter in it. Explain that the one who gets the red counter will be the 'killer' but must not give the game away. Collect the envelopes and tell the children the game can start. The object is for the 'killer' to 'kill' other people by winking at them, while the rest of the children try to guess who it is. They must be quite skilful as they have to watch other people without accidentally making eye-contact with the 'killer' and therefore ending up 'dead'. Usually children cheat!
- ball games: stand in a circle and throw a soft ball to each other, but not in any sequence;
- 'Pass the Parcel': this encourages children to be attentive and to maintain their attention in a group;
- variations on 'Pass the Parcel': for example, pass a piece of clothing around the circle, and when the music stops the child puts it on; keep doing this until everyone is dressed up;

◆ 'Pass the Hat Round': sit in a circle and sing this song:

> Pass the hat round
> pass it round
> pass it round
> pass it round,
> pass the hat round
> pass it round,
> and put it on your head.

The child holding the hat at this point puts it on. You can continue till everyone has worn the hat, or introduce different items, such as sunglasses, a scarf, a shiny wig, and so on, changing the words accordingly.

TACTILE GAMES
Table Top

You will need:

one set of tactile dominoes; these can be bought or made at home out of various materials, such as hessian, sandpaper, velvet, smooth cord, corduroy, and so on.

Useful words and phrases:

dominoes; play(ing); same; different; touch; finish(ed); winner; can't go; names of materials used on the dominoes; names of textures, such as rough, smooth, and so on.

What to do

1 Sit at the table.

2 Play as for any dominoes game but encourage the child to feel the textures. You can only put down dominoes that match in texture. The first person to lay all their pieces down is the winner.

Variations

◆ Use more or fewer dominoes.

◆ Make the textures more similar.

◆ Make dominoes that have similar textures but different materials, such as smooth ones made from silk and satin; rough ones made from hessian and sandpaper; and so on.

◆ Play the game blindfolded to really concentrate on the tactile experience; in a group it is better for you to remain unblindfolded so you can keep control of the game and make sure the children are matching the correct textures — or you can let them finish the game, and then check for themselves how they got on.

Similar activities

You can find or make games and activities that encourage attention to touch and textures. Many are available in ordinary shops; some from educational catalogues. For example:

◆ tactile matching and discrimination games (find textures that feel the same or different);

◆ texture lotto (play as any lotto, but with scraps of material instead of pictures — try not to give other clues through colours and patterns);

◆ make tactile books;

◆ Fuzzy-Felt Pictures (available from many toy shops);

◆ textured pictures: make your own with scraps of material;

◆ collages;

◆ matching raised or textured shapes, letters and numbers;

◆ tactile memory games: 'Pelmanism': make cards with different textures on one side, turn them all face-down, and you have to find matching pairs; or give the child a texture to feel, then remove it and ask her to find the one that matches, from a choice on the table.

TACTILE GAMES
Feelie-Bags

What to do

1. Show the child the objects, and let her feel each one in turn, encouraging her to use both hands. Name each object.

2. Hide the objects and put one of them into the bag without the child seeing. (A screen is useful for hiding the rest of the objects.)

3. Ask her to put her hands inside the bag, feel the object and, without looking, say what it is.

4. Let her see if she is right.

5. Repeat the game with different objects.

Variations

◆ Put more objects in the bag: the more there are, the harder it is; the child can still feel only one item, or she can feel all of them, and see how many she gets right.

◆ Vary the objects in the bag, perhaps making them more similar.

◆ Instead of a bag use a box, which makes it slightly easier, as a box is more rigid; you could also have several boxes, with a different object in each one.

◆ Instead of feeling inside the bag, the child must feel the object *through* the bag, which is much harder; start with a bag made of thin material and only one object inside, and gradually make it more difficult.

◆ It is even harder to play by touch only, that is without seeing the objects first.

◆ Put all the objects in the bag, describe one, and ask the child to find it.

◆ Show the child an object which matches one of those in the bag or box and ask her to find it.

◆ In a group, let each child feel the same object before pulling it from the bag to see what it is, so that they can compare their performances.

◆ Make a competition out of it, each child scoring points.

You will need:

a large non-see-through bag (material is better than plastic); three or four common objects (easily recognized by feel, but very different from each other, such as a ball, cup, pencil, small teddy bear); a screen (optional).

Useful words and phrases:

feelie-bag; touch; feel; handle; hide; hidden; guess; right; wrong; names of objects in the bag.

S E C T I O N 5

Similar activities

You can carry out the same activity with all sorts of things in the bag. One idea is to group the objects into categories. For example:

◆ toys;

◆ household items;

◆ coins;

◆ things to eat;

◆ nature items;

◆ different textures;

◆ pieces of material;

◆ school items;

◆ shapes.

You can also find similar games in educational catalogues and some high street shops.

 Beware of putting sharp objects in the bag!

TACTILE GAMES
Quizzes

What to do

1 Show the child all the objects you are going to use, and let her feel each one in turn, encouraging her to use both hands. Name each object.

2 Go out of sight and put four to six of the objects on a tray. (A screen is useful for hiding behind.)

3 Blindfold the child and ask her to feel all the objects on the tray and name each one. Write down what she says.

4 When she has finished, take off the blindfold and let her see all the objects, then report back on how well she got on. Award one point for each item correct.

Variations

◆ Put more or fewer objects on the tray to make the game harder or easier.

◆ Vary the objects on the tray, perhaps making them more similar: for example, use very small items such as shells, rice and pasta.

◆ It is much harder to play the game by touch only: that is, without seeing the objects first.

◆ Describe one of the objects on the tray, and ask the child to find it.

◆ Place an object that exactly matches one of the objects on the tray into her hands; do not tell her what it is, but ask her to find the same thing from the tray. To make it harder, ask her to find two or three matching objects.

◆ Play 'Kim's Game': the child has to say which object is missing. Let her see and feel everything on the tray, then take one

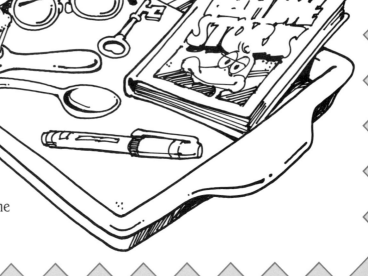

You will need:

one blindfold; several common objects (easily recognized by feel, but very different from each other, such as a pair of glasses, a brush, a book, a pen, a spoon); a tray; a screen (optional).

Useful words and phrases:

quiz; blindfold; touch; feel; handle; guess; hide; missing; same.

129

thing away. To make it harder ask her to close her eyes or blindfold her first; or take away more than one object; or move the rest of the objects around.

◆ In a group, you may need to change some of the objects on the tray, so that the last children do not benefit from the others' attempts; or the tray could be hidden until the last child has had her turn; then see who got the most right.

◆ Give a small reward to each child who got all the items correct, or to the one with the most right.

Similar activities

You can carry out the same basic activity using all sorts of things. One idea is to group the objects into categories. You can also use people and objects in the room, leading the child from one to another. For example:

◆ toys;
◆ coins;
◆ household items;
◆ school items;
◆ things to eat;
◆ nature items;
◆ people;
◆ clothing;
◆ parts of the room.

You could also place each object in an individual bag and ask the child to match up the bags; if you are using categories, the child could try and find the odd one out.

TACTILE GAMES
Party Games

What to do

1 Clear away all breakable objects from the play area.

2 Make the play area safe, with nothing to trip over or bump into.

3 Get the children into a circle, then blindfold one child and stand her in the middle.

4 Lead the blindfolded child to one of the children, whom she must identify by feel.

5 When she has guessed, if she is right, take the blindfold off and let her see the other child. If she is wrong, allow one more guess, after helping her to feel identifying features, such as glasses, long hair or a bracelet.

6 The two children swap places, and the game is repeated until everyone has had a go.

Variations

◆ After you have blindfolded the child in the middle, get some of the others to *quietly* change places.

◆ Spin the blindfolded child around, instead of making the others change places.

◆ Each child can go round feeling everybody to see how many they get right (it usually gets easier by a process of elimination).

◆ If you have a bigger space, the children can move around, so that the 'Blindman' has to catch somebody before identifying them; then either they swap places or each correctly identified person has to go and sit down, until everybody has been caught, and another 'Blindman' is chosen.

Similar activities

◆ 'Pin-the-Tail-on-the-Donkey': you will need a large picture of a donkey with a detachable tail (use a piece of Blu-Tack or Hold-it, as a pin might hurt). Make the donkey with strong material and a raised outline (for example from string), as the point is to encourage the children to feel where to put the tail, not just guess wildly. Each child has a turn and the one who gets nearest wins.

You will need:

for 'Blindman's Buff',
a blindfold; several
children and/or adults.

Useful words
and phrases:

blindfold; can't see;
feel; touch; who; names
of other children; names
of body parts, clothing
and personal items.

- ◆ Variations on the above: 'Pin-the-Head-on-the-Lady'; 'Pin-the-Roof-on-the-House'; 'Pin-the-Wheel-on-the-Car'; 'Pin-the-Nose-on-the-Face'; 'Pin-the-Trunk-on-the-Elephant'.
- ◆ 'Sardines': in this game, everybody goes to hide, except one child who counts to ten and then goes to look for them. However, the idea is to squash as many children into the same hiding place as possible. When the child has found all the children, someone else is appointed 'It'. A variation of this game is for one child to go and hide while everybody else looks. The first child to find the hiding child hides with her, and so on, until the last child finds all the other children hiding in the same place. These games usually lead to lots of giggling in an effort to keep quiet.
- ◆ 'Guess-the-Parcel': loosely wrap several objects so that you can feel what is inside but not too easily. Put a number on each parcel and keep a record of what is inside. You can play this as a quiz, with the children guessing what is in each parcel and you keeping a record of how many each child gets right. Or you can play it as 'Pass-the-Parcel', passing it round to the music and feeling and guessing when the music stops. Keep playing until someone guesses correctly. Afterwards, they can unwrap the parcels, and the winners get a small reward.
- ◆ 'Bran Tubs/Lucky Dips': this involves feeling for 'prizes' in a tub of sawdust or something similar. You can also wrap the 'prizes' following their actual shapes and see if the child can guess what they are.

TASTE GAMES
Quizzes

What to do

1 Blindfold the child, or ask her to close her eyes.

2 Give her a taste of one of the foods, and ask her to identify it, and say whether she likes it or not. Make a note of her answers.

3 Continue with all the other tastes, writing down the responses. Have a drink of water ready if needed.

4 Afterwards, take the blindfold off and show the child how many she got right.

Variations

◆ Show the child the foods before she begins to taste them; this makes it easier to identify them and also gives her a chance to take out anything she really doesn't like.

◆ Ask the child to identify the type of taste or texture — sweet or sour, smooth or crunchy, and so on.

◆ Give the child one item of food to taste, without saying what it is, and then ask her to find the same one, from a choice of two or more.

◆ Carry out the activity with the child holding her nose to cut out her sense of smell, and discuss the difference it makes.

◆ This can also be played in a group, as a team game.

Similar activities

The same activity could be carried out using all sorts of different foods and drinks, including herbs and spices, and so on. It is harder, however, to identify mixed foods, for example, to expect the child to identify garlic in garlic-flavoured mashed potato, and so on.

In a group, the activity could lead to a discussion about different food groups, ethnic dishes, health and nutrition and the children's favourite foods. For example:

Food groups:
◆ breads;
◆ cakes and biscuits;
◆ fruits;
◆ vegetables;

You will need:

several different kinds of familiar foods, such as chocolates, tomato sauce, sugar, salt, bread, grated cheese, lemon curd, and so on; several spoons; a box of tissues for wiping the children's mouths; a jug of water and beakers; one blindfold (or put each item of food into an unlabelled, numbered container, and keep a record of which food is in each one).

Useful words and phrases:

food; taste; try; tongue; nose; smell; like; don't like; names of flavours.

133

- meats;
- fish;
- dairy produce;
- herbs;
- condiments and spices;
- drinks;
- spreads;
- desserts;
- cereals.

Ethnic foods and national dishes:
- curries;
- Chinese food;
- Mexican food and chillies;
- Caribbean fruits;
- Asian fruits and vegetables;
- Greek and Turkish dishes;
- paella;
- various Italian pastas;
- Scandinavian smorgasbord;
- German sausages;
- Swiss fondue.

Health and nutrition:
- healthy foods;
- less healthy foods;
- nutritional properties of food;
- foods that should be avoided (but may be eaten in small quantities);
- balanced diets;
- foods that may give allergies.

TASTE GAMES
Role-Play Games

What to do

1 Set up the 'shop' with the foods on display. Choose foods that can be tasted easily and immediately once 'bought'.

2 You will be the shopkeeper; the child will be the customer.

3 The child chooses what to buy, takes it 'home' and eats it (under your supervision).

4 Discuss the different foods and tastes.

Variations

◆ This game can be made as simple or elaborate as you want, by adding props and extra 'pretend' activities.

◆ You can give the game a listening dimension by telling the child which foods she has to buy.

◆ Add a matching element by giving her a shopping list made from pictures or symbols.

◆ Introduce a literacy element by writing the shopping list down.

◆ The game can be adapted for a group of children taking different roles, for example shopkeeper, different customers, delivery person, and so on.

◆ You could add a 'taster' bar in the shop, where the children have to say if they like the taste of a 'new' food.

Similar activities

Similar games to encourage tasting include the following:

◆ 'Picnic': act out having a picnic and take your favourite foods to taste;

◆ 'Monster Feast': pretend to be strange creatures and monsters and take your least favourite foods to taste;

◆ 'Party': pretend to have a party, where you try out 'new' foods (that is, less familiar ones);

◆ 'Restaurants': act out being diners, chefs, waiters and waitresses, and order your favourite foods from the menus;

◆ 'Midnight Feast': turn the lights out, pull the curtains and eat by torchlight. Be naughty!

You will need:

for 'Shopping Game':
'pretend' shop; real foods to 'buy'; shopping bags; shopping list (optional); till (optional); toy money (optional).

Useful words and phrases:

shop; shopping; buy; home; eat; taste; like; don't like; names of foods.

◆ 'TV Cooks': pretend to be on television food shows, cooking, eating and drinking; have tasting panels to judge food and drinks;

◆ 'Stories': read a book, such as *The Very Hungry Caterpillar*, or make up a similar story, and taste all the real foods mentioned in the text; discuss the flavours and textures and the implications of eating so many foods;

◆ 'Treasure Hunt': hide pictures of food around the room or garden, then give clues to what they are and where to find them: for example, "I'm small, red and sweet. You'll find me in a basket." Answer: a strawberry. When the child has found all the pictures, she can taste the foods.

Note: These games are even more fun when played by groups of children.

SMELL GAMES
Quizzes & Games

What to do

1 Blindfold the child, or ask her to close her eyes.

2 Let her smell one of the jars, then ask her to identify the scent and say whether she likes it or not. Make a note of her answers.

3 Continue with all the other smells, writing down her responses.

4 Afterwards, take the blindfold off and show her how many she got right.

Variations

◆ Show the child the substances before she begins to smell them — this makes it easier.

◆ Match up bottles with the same smells.

◆ Cotton-wool buds or tissues can be dipped in different smelling substances, or scented strips can be used, as an alternative to jars and bottles.

◆ You can buy 'smelly' badges, cards and pictures, which release their scent when rubbed.

◆ This can also be played in a group, as a team game.

Similar activities

◆ Make books and stories more interesting by having the appropriate aromas to smell at relevant points; books about food, gardens and specific events, such as a fireworks display, having a bubble-bath, and so on, would be suitable.

◆ Make 'smelly' pictures and books, by soaking material in the scent you want, or using dried flowers, sandalwood, soapstone, and so on.

◆ Match the smells to pictures — the smell of wood to a picture of a tree; the smell of butter to a picture of butter, and so on.

You will need:

for a quiz: several different smells, for example small bottles or jars containing aromas such as lavender, lilac, rose, and so on; a blindfold (optional).

Useful words and phrases:

smell; try; nose; like; don't like; names of aromas.

SECTION 5

TOPICS

SECTION 6

INTRODUCTION

THIS SECTION is aimed at older or more able children, who have some expressive language skills and can take some part in discussions. Many of the games and activities also demand a high degree of mobility and manipulation skills.

We learn about the world and the things in it more quickly if we can touch them and handle them. Children like to explore and experiment, and much of this is done by using their hands, so the sense of touch has an obvious part to play in learning.

These activities are most suitable for children in school, to help them learn more about their environment by using sight, touch, taste and smell. Most of the activities are best carried out in small groups, so that children can experience working co-operatively and using language for a variety of purposes. However, they may also be used in individual teaching sessions in schools and therapy clinics.

The section starts with some general ideas to vary activities. Then there are three specific topics which highlight the senses of sight and touch. Next, examples are given of the way touch, taste and smell can contribute to children's learning and enjoyment of five common topics. Finally, there are some suggestions for using touch, taste and smell in the core school curriculum subjects of Maths, Science and English.

Aims

1 To have fun.

2 To raise the child's awareness of, and interest in, the senses of sight, touch, taste and smell.

3 To help the child learn about the world.

4 To make learning about topics more realistic and interesting, by varying the activities and experiences.

5 To teach appropriate vocabulary.

6 To use language for a variety of purposes, such as finding out, reporting back, discussing, and so on.

7 To encourage interaction and communication between children.

8 To encourage co-operative working.

Remember!

◆ We learn about the world and the things in it more quickly if we can touch them and handle them.

◆ These topics are for older and more able children, who can take some part in discussions.

◆ Many of the games and activities need good mobility and manipulation skills.

◆ These activities are most suitable for children in school or other environments where they can work in small groups.

TOPICS
General Ideas

Use a range of activities when teaching topics. Vary seated activities with lively ones, primarily language-based activities with more practical ones, and so on. For example:

◆ discussions;
◆ stories;
◆ quizzes;
◆ role-plays, acting out situations;
◆ games;
◆ surveys;
◆ spot what's wrong in the picture or story;
◆ videos;
◆ art and craft;
◆ physical activities and games;
◆ making books and writing;
◆ educational visits.

Specific topics
The following examples show how children can be made more aware of the senses of sight and touch.

Examples of activities

◆ Discuss why we need our eyes.

◆ Experience what it is like to see nothing (and maybe hear nothing) for three minutes.

◆ Try doing everyday activities without using the eyes: wear a blindfold and start with very simple things such as touching your own nose; go on to slightly harder ones such as walking around the room, finding a favourite toy from the toy-box or cupboard, eating a sweet or piece of fruit. Difficult activities are finding or identifying a particular person, finding the way to a specified place within the house or school, getting dressed. Try impossible activities, too, to really bring home the point: for example, reading a book, watching television, describing what someone is doing.

◆ Experience what it is like to have other people do things for you, or to you; for example, being guided around, being fed, having your face washed.

◆ Make a list of what we would miss, or find very difficult, if we could not see: for example, colours, shapes and patterns; seeing what friends and family look like; watching television and films; looking at photos, pictures and books; appreciating art and sculpture; following fashion.

◆ Discuss whether there are any other ways to make up for not seeing: for example, using the sense of touch to feel people's faces, the shape of sculptures and the texture of clothes; listening to the sound of animals and birds, to people's voices and to 'talking books'; smelling flowers and food.

◆ Discuss how important the other senses become.

◆ Discuss what dangers there might be and how these might be overcome: for example, crossing the road; coping with uneven pavements and obstacles in the street or around the house; knowing when food has gone mouldy.

◆ Have a discussion about blind and partially-sighted people. Who suffers? How do we lose our sight? What are the effects of blindness from infancy compared to acquired blindness?

Examples of activities

◆ Discuss why we need our hands.

◆ Try doing things without using the hands: simple activities, such as walking, sitting on the floor and getting up again, drinking through a straw; harder activities, such as eating, reading, painting, peeling a banana; impossible or almost impossible activities, such as doing up shoelaces, doing up buttons, writing, scratching your back.

◆ How important do other parts of our body become when we cannot use our hands? What else can we use?

◆ Have a discussion about disabled/physically handicapped people: think of examples of the difficulties faced and how these can be overcome.

◆ Try doing things with the eyes closed or pretend to be blind: how important does touch become? (Make sure the area is safe and you have removed any dangerous obstacles for this activity.)

◆ Discuss visual disability: think of examples of difficulties faced and how these can be overcome. For example, how do blind people choose their clothes?

◆ Close your eyes and concentrate on what your body can feel: different parts of your body, the feel of your clothes, the chair, your feet on the floor, the breeze, how warm it is, and so on.

◆ Experience being blindfolded and 'deafened': put earplugs in the ears or wear headphones with music to block out people's speech. Experience what it is like to have other people do things to you while you are like this, such as washing, feeding, leading you around. See how important the way we touch each other is.

◆ What does touch tell us? How do we touch when we feel angry, happy, miserable? How do we touch others if we are strangers, friends, family? Discuss touch and privacy; touch and affection.

 If you are helping children to experience being 'blind' or 'deaf', make sure you supervise them well, and escort them wherever they go.

Don't Touch

Examples of activities

◆ Discuss how touching and tasting can have dangers.

◆ You can talk about the dangers of different groups of objects and how they may harm us. For example:

  sharp objects, broken glass (cuts);
  hot objects, fires, kettles, cookers, matches (burns);
  electrical appliances, plugs, wires, sockets (shocks);
  bleach, poisons, household cleaners (burns, sickness);
  rotten food, undercooked food (sickness);
  animals, other people's pets (bites, attacks);
  people, good touch, bad touch (attacks, sexual abuse).

◆ Discuss how to avoid difficult situations, but also what to do in emergencies.

◆ Discuss the nature of public behaviour and private behaviour, and what the child should do if she does not want to be touched.

◆ Discuss the nature of pain and sickness, and how to tell people what is wrong.

(!) Some of these topics can be sensitive issues, especially where they touch on sexual behaviour, and you must be clear about the message you are giving. It is worth repeating the warning given in previous sections, to make sure that nothing you say or do could be construed as improper behaviour. Always follow the guidelines of the school you are working in.

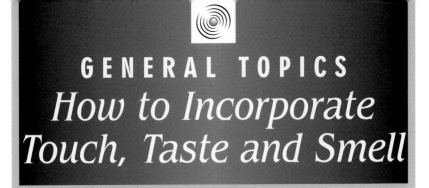

How to Incorporate Touch, Taste and Smell

Touch, taste and smell can be included in many classroom topics, because they bring home to children the real experience of what they are learning. When you are planning a topic, think about ways of including sensory activities, both for fun and for educational purposes. The following examples show how touch, taste and smell can be used to reinforce some common topics.

SECTION 6

GENERAL TOPICS 1
Animals

Examples of activities

◆ Stroke pets, farm animals and children's zoo animals (under supervision).

◆ Visit a museum to see and feel fur, feathers, snake skin, and so on.

◆ Make collages of animals with realistic textures.

◆ Make animal pictures from textures and materials.

◆ Play with cuddly toys and plush toy animals.

◆ Use Fuzzy-Felt animal pictures.

◆ Make balloon animal shapes.

◆ Model animals from clay, Soft Stuff, and so on.

◆ Make animal-shaped biscuits and sweets.

◆ Smell animal habitats, straw, animal foods (but do not encourage tasting).

◆ Ride different animals.

◆ Discuss what animals we eat, and what the meat is called.

◆ Collect wool, feathers, and so on — only those shed naturally, not taken from live animals, of course.

◆ Visit an aquarium that has supervised areas where children can feel certain fish, such as skate and ray, and other sea creatures.

(!) Observe all rules about safety and hygiene, whether they are commonsense rules, or the specific policies of your school or the place you are visiting.

GENERAL TOPICS 2
The Weather

Examples of activities

◆ Experience different types of weather: go out in the sun, rain, wind, snow, sleet, hail, warm weather, cold weather, very hot weather. Smell the difference in the air after rain.

◆ Simulate different types of weather, using a hair-drier for warm wind, an air-conditioning fan for cold wind, a plant-sprayer for rain, a sun-ray lamp for the sun, ice-cubes, cut up extremely small, for hail, and so on.

◆ Discuss how different parts of the body react to different temperatures and suffer varying amounts of heat loss.

◆ Discuss the importance of keeping warm (clothing, heating, and so on) and how the cold affects the elderly.

◆ Experience how different clothes feel in different environments and temperatures — the discomfort of heavy woollen jumpers on hot days, and so on.

◆ Contrast the climates of different countries and simulate these conditions.

 Observe all safety and hygiene rules. Make sure nobody gets too hot, cold or wet for too long. Have plenty of towels and a warm environment on hand.

SECTION 6

GENERAL TOPICS 3
Town & Country

Examples of activities

◆ Compare the town environment with the countryside and discuss what you expect to find.

◆ In the town, feel the textures of buildings and the materials of the environment, such as bricks, concrete and glass, and see how they retain heat or stay cold.

◆ In the country, feel the textures of the environment, for example hedges, grass, mud and tree bark.

◆ Contrast the precise geometrical shapes of the man-made environment with those that occur in nature.

◆ Discuss the different smells of town and country, such as car exhausts, fish and chip shops and so on, versus cow manure, flowers and 'fresh' air.

◆ Build models reflecting the different shapes and textures.

GENERAL TOPICS 4
Different Countries

Examples of activities

◆ Buy, cook and eat fruits and vegetables from different countries: kiwi fruit, passion fruit, mango, banana, okra, sweet potato, yam and so on. Feel, smell and taste them first.

◆ Cook well-known dishes from different countries. For example:

Chilli con carne (Mexico)
Chicken korma (India)
Rice and peas (Caribbean)
Paella (Spain)
Spaghetti bolognese (Italy)
Haggis (Scotland)
Bortsch (Russia)
Hamburger (USA)
Shepherd's pie (Great Britain)

◆ Go out to restaurants specializing in foreign foods.

◆ Wear and feel the traditional costumes of different countries, paying attention to the textures and types of clothes worn for different weather conditions. Some museums allow such educational visits and encourage touching the exhibits and trying on the clothes.

◆ Recreate the climates of different countries.

◆ Recreate the traditional houses: what does a tepee feel like? How cold is an igloo? Again, museums are good places to experience these.

◆ Visit botanical gardens and other places where you can see, touch and smell plants and trees from other lands.

◆ Visit zoos and safari parks where you can see, and maybe touch, animals from other lands.

◆ Grow your own plants, flowers, herbs and spices from other lands, especially those which have an interesting texture or distinctive smell.

GENERAL TOPICS 5
Fruit

Examples of activities

◆ Discuss and name different fruits.

◆ Go shopping for a variety of fruits, noting the more exotic ones to be found in the shops nowadays.

◆ Feel the outside of the different fruits and compare their textures.

◆ Smell the fruits: whole, and when cut open.

◆ Taste the insides and outsides of the fruits and compare flavours.

◆ Feel and taste the fruits raw and cooked; hot and cold.

◆ Discuss the children's favourites; do a survey and make a graph or chart to show the results.

◆ Make nutrition charts and posters.

◆ Make posters using pictures of the fruits.

◆ Make 'feelie' pictures and posters, using the washed and dried skins of the fruits. (They will not last long, though — throw them out before they get smelly or mouldy.)

Examples of fruits:

Apple; pear; cherry; pineapple; grapes; kiwi fruit; ugli fruit; banana; mango; guava; orange; passion fruit; star fruit; lemon; lychee; tangerine; pomegranate.

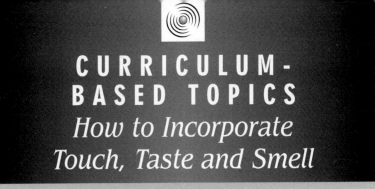

CURRICULUM-BASED TOPICS
How to Incorporate Touch, Taste and Smell

We learn about the world and the things in it more quickly if we can touch them and handle them. Children like to explore and experiment, and much of this is done by using their hands. The following examples show how touch, taste and smell can be used in teaching the core subjects of a school curriculum. It was not thought necessary to include visual activities as they are already an integral part of teaching.

Remember!

◆ These activities are aimed at older or more able children who have some expressive language skills and can take some part in discussions.

◆ Good mobility and manipulation skills are needed for many of the activities.

◆ They are best carried out in small groups.

© Jackie Cooke 1996
You may photocopy this page for instructional use only

Children can learn about the properties of shapes more quickly by feeling them, in both a three-dimensional and a two-dimensional form. You can make shapes and numbers from textured materials, which helps children to learn and recall them better. (See also p 80 for ideas on exploring shapes.)

When children trace the outline of shapes and numbers with their fingers, it often helps them to remember how to draw or write them later on.

Touch can also be used as a counting aid. It is easier to keep track of where you are if you touch each object as you count it. Counting is also easier if the objects are put into straight rows, rather than left higgledy-piggledy.

Tasting can be used as a motivator. For example, it is far more interesting to count things if they are sweets that you can eat afterwards!

CURRICULUM-BASED TOPICS 2
Science

Touch, taste and smell probably have more obvious applications to science. For instance, practical sensory experiences are vital when learning about the body, particularly the senses, in both humans and other animals.

Sensory experiences are also useful when learning about other topics, such as the weather, the environment, temperature, water, how things grow, food and flavours, clothing and textiles, rubbish and pollution, the home, and so on. (Also see some of the ideas for General Topics.)

Touching and handling are also essential when conducting scientific experiments and when learning about the properties of objects, such as shape, size and weight.

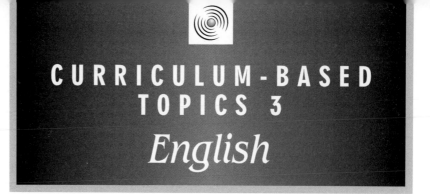

CURRICULUM-BASED TOPICS 3
English

Children learn about objects and events in the environment more quickly if they can use all their senses, with touching and handling being particularly important. Even in later life we value 'hands-on' experience. Imagine how difficult it would be to learn a practical activity such as driving in a purely theoretical way. The sense of touch therefore contributes both directly and indirectly to cognitive and language development.

Children learn and recall the names of objects more quickly if they can handle and use them. When you teach a child the name of an object, such as a ball, do not just show her the ball: play with it, touch, feel and throw it, and so on.

The experiences of touching, tasting and smelling are vital when teaching the vocabulary associated with these senses. Words like 'soft', 'hard', 'spicy', 'salty', 'smelly', and so on, would be very difficult to teach without using sensory activities.

Specific activities are also useful in literacy skills. For example, touch is very important to young children in their early appreciation of books. They like turning the pages, touching the pictures, having textures to feel and flaps to lift. Some books for young children are made from material, foam and thick board, to encourage their interest and make it easy for them to turn the pages by themselves. The range of such books in the shops is quite limited, but you can make your own quite easily, with the children choosing the textures. You can also attach real (small) objects or pictures of objects to home-made books. The children can handle them or match them to the story or picture-book.

Like numbers, the written form of letters may be more easily learnt and reproduced by feeling raised or textured shapes. Tracing the shape of the letters with the finger is also a traditional aid to letter recognition and writing.

APPENDICES

APPENDIX I
Basic Resources for Sensory Activities

This appendix lists toys, objects and materials that you can easily collect and store together for use with basic sensory activities. The idea is to keep a box of the most useful ones always handy:

◆ bright or colourful mobile;
◆ torch;
◆ face paints;
◆ medium-sized mirror;
◆ shiny wig or floppy hat;
◆ small clockwork toys;
◆ *Koosh* ball
◆ hand-held fans, battery-operated mini-fans;
◆ bubbles, water-spray;
◆ variety of brushes (thick and thin);
◆ variety of materials (from light, eg. silk, to heavy, eg. carpet);
◆ variety of textures (soft, rough, smooth, scratchy);
◆ creams, talcs and lip balm;
◆ perfume and after-shave;
◆ aromatic oils.

Also have some interesting tastes and food-essences available, but keep them in the appropriate storage conditions and always check the date by which they should be used.

Lastly, fill some jars with soft sand or flour, dried peas, rice or pasta shapes — old coffee jars or sweet jars will do — and keep one clean tray or washing-up bowl for the child to explore them in.

(!) **Please remember the various warnings given with the activities about children's health, hygiene, safety and so on. Always supervise your child when using these toys and materials.**

APPENDIX II
Songs, Rhymes and Hand-games

This appendix gives the words and actions of the hand-games and songs referred to in the text. They can be used either as tactile games, with you carrying out the actions on the child, or as visual games, with the child copying you, whichever is appropriate.

Look in children's bookshops and toyshops for other suitable songs and rhymes. There are many collections of nursery rhymes, some with accompanying audio tapes. One good source is: Ian Beck and Sarah Williams, *Round and Round the Garden, play rhymes for young children*, Oxford University Press, Oxford, 1994 edition. This book has illustrations that show how to carry out the actions. There is also a companion tape containing the tunes and the words to the songs. Other titles in the series (1994 editions) are: Ian Beck and Karen King, *Oranges and Lemons, singing and dancing games;* Ian Beck and Sarah Williams, *Pudding and Pie, favourite nursery rhymes.*

Hand-games

'Here's the church, here's the steeple'

Words	Actions
Here's the church	Put your hands together with the fingers interlocking palm side and pointing downwards
Here's the steeple	Raise the two first fingers, and touch fingertips
Come inside	Turn your hands over so that the child can see your fingers
And see the people	Wiggle your fingers

'Tommy Thumb'

Words	Action
Tommy thumb	
Tommy thumb	
Where are you?	
Here I am	Wave your thumb or the child's
Here I am	thumb in the air
And how do you do?	

Repeat with the fingers. The first finger is 'Peter Pointer', the middle is 'Middle Man', the third is 'Ruby Ring' and the little finger is 'Baby Small'. The last verse goes:

Fingers all
Fingers all
Where are you?
Here we are

Here we are
And how do you do?

'Two little dickie-birds sitting on a wall'

Words	*Actions*
Two little dickie-birds sitting on a wall	Wiggle the first fingers of both hands
One named Peter, one named Paul	Wiggle one finger, then the other
Fly away Peter, fly away Paul	Make each finger 'fly' away
Come back Peter, come back Paul	Make each finger come back

Songs and Rhymes

'This little piggy went to market'

This little piggy went to market
This little piggy stayed at home
This little piggy had roast beef
This little piggy had none
But this little piggy went …
Weeee — all the way home
Actions: Tickle or pull a toe as you say the lines, and end up by tickling the child in a ticklish place.

'Pat-a-cake, pat-a-cake, baker's man'

Pat-a-cake, pat-a-cake, baker's man
Bake me a cake as fast as you can
Roll it and pat it and mark it with 'B'
And put it in the oven for Baby and me
Actions: Alternate between clapping the child's hands and your own. Make up a sequence, such as own hands, both child's hands, child's left hand, child's right hand, own hands.

'One finger, one thumb, keep moving'

(1st verse)   One finger, one thumb, keep moving
One finger, one thumb, keep moving
One finger, one thumb, keep moving
We'll all be merry and bright or Keep moving all day long
(2nd verse)   One finger, one thumb, one arm, keep moving … etc
(3rd verse)   One finger, one thumb, one arm, one leg, keep moving … etc
(4th verse)   One finger, one thumb, one arm, one leg,

one nod of the head, keep moving … etc

(5th verse) One finger, one thumb, one arm, one leg, one nod of the head, stand up, sit down, keep moving … etc

Actions: Touch, stroke or shake the child's finger, thumb, arm and leg. Carry out the other actions on the child according to the song. You can also make up your own.

'Shake my hand'

Shake my hand
Shake my hand
Hello … (child's name)
Shake my hand

Action: Shake the child's hand as you sing.

'Incy-wincy spider'

(1st verse) Incy-wincy spider
Climbed up the spout
Down came the rain
And washed the spider out

Actions: Make slow, spidery movements going up in the air, then a quick downwards movement.

(2nd verse) Out came the sun
And dried up all the rain
And Incy-wincy spider
Climbed up the spout again

Actions: Make a flourish like the sun coming out, and 'walk' the spider up again.

'Wind the bobbin up'

Wind the bobbin up
Wind the bobbin up
Pull, pull, pull
Point to the ceiling
Point to the floor
Point to the window
Point to the door
Clap your hands together
One, two, three
Put your hands upon your knee

Actions: Make circles with your hands going around each other for the winding movements. The rest is self-explanatory.

APPENDIX II
Songs, Rhymes and Hand-games

'Wheels on the bus'

(1st verse)   The wheels on the bus go round and round
Round and round
Round and round
The wheels on the bus go round and round
All day long

(2nd verse)   The wipers on the bus go swish, swish, swish ... etc

(3rd verse)   The bell on the bus goes ding, ding, ding ... etc

(4th verse)   The children on the bus go chatter, chatter, chatter ... etc

(5th verse)   The driver on the bus says "Tickets please" ... etc

Actions: Make circles with your hands for the wheels. Mime the other actions according to the words. You can also make up your own words and actions.

'Roly-poly'

(1st verse)   Roly-poly, roly-poly, round and round
Roly-poly, roly-poly, round and round
Roly-poly, roly-poly, round and round
And clap your hands together — one, two, three

(2nd verse)   Shaker, shaker, shaker, shaker, up and down ... etc

(3rd verse)   Wibble-wobble, wibble-wobble, side-to-side ... etc

Actions: Move your hands around in circles in the first verse, shake them up and down in the second verse and shake your body from side to side in the third verse. Clap as appropriate.

Shops

United Kingdom

Early Learning Centre This high street shop provides very good value toys and activities, which are both educational and fun. You can pick up a catalogue from the shops themselves. There is also a mail order service:
Mail Order Dept
Early Learning Centre
South Marston Park
Swindon SN3 4TJ
www.elc.co.uk

Toys 'Я' Us These are large toy stores, usually found on the edge of towns, in retail parks. Along with the commercial toys they also sell products such as activity centres and 'feelie' quilts for babies, good cause and effect and visual toys, and one-off gems such as a glittery pom-pom. They also sell large active toys for the home, such as ball pools, trampolines and slides.
www.toysrus.com

Children's World This is another large store, along similar lines to the one above.
www.childrensworld.com

Woolworths This high street store sells inexpensive toys, amongst which you will find some useful novelty toys. This is also a good place to buy Christmas garlands, tinsel, balloons, and so on.
www.woolworths.co.uk

United States of America

Didax, Inc
395 Main Street
Rowley
MA 01969
www.didaxinc.com

Incentives for Learning
111 Center Avenue
Suite 1
Pacheco
CA 94553
www.incentivesforlearning.com

FAO Schwarz A chain of children's stores found throughout the USA.
www.fao.com

Pro-Ed
8700 Shoal Creek Blvd
Austin
TX 78757-6897
www.proedinc.com

S&S Worldwide
75 Mill Street
PO Box 513
Colchester
CT 06415
www.ssww.com

The Speech Bin
1965 Twenty-Fifth Avenue
Vero Beach
FL 32960
www.speechbin.com

Super Duper Publications
PO Box 24997
Greenville
SC 29616
www.superduperinc.com

Toys 'Я' Us
A chain of children's stores found throughout the USA.
www.toysrus.com

Zany Brainy
3342 Melrose Ave NW
Roanoke
VA 24017
www.zanybrainy.com

Mail Order

United Kingdom

Innovations A division of Argos, this company produces innovative toys and gifts. There are a lot of little inexpensive gadgets and toys, such as giant bubble makers, glowing yo-yos, fibre-optic torches and Newton's cradles. Catalogues from:

ARG Equation Ltd
19th Floor
Arndale Centre
Market Street
Manchester M60 6EQ
www.innovations.co.uk

Speechmark Publishing Ltd (formerly *Winslow Press*)
This company publishes ColorCards® and many books describing language and play activities, which both parents and professionals will find useful. A catalogue is available:

Speechmark Publishing Ltd
Telford Road
Bicester
Oxon OX26 4LQ
www.speechmark.net

APPENDIX III
Useful Addresses and Resources

TFH (formerly *Toys for the Handicapped*) This is particularly useful for tactile toys and large visual toys which are strong and sturdy, and especially designed for children with special needs. Catalogues from:

TFH
5–7 Severnside Business Park
Stourport-on-Severn
Worcestershire DY13 9HT
www.tfhuk.com

!Tridias! This company produces good-value toys and materials, such as the *Playnest*, which is an inflatable ring for a baby to sit in and play with the toys that are attached. Their 'stocking fillers' section is a good source of cheap visual toys, which light up, sparkle and so on. However do not expect them to be long-lasting if they are used with lots of children. Mail order service:

Tridias, Customer Services
The Buffer Depot
Badminton Road
Acton Turville
Gloucestershire GL9 1HE
www.tridias.co.uk

United States of America

TFH (USA) Ltd
4537 Gibsonia Rd
Gibsonia
PA 15044
www.tfhusa.com